THE **22**

Biggest Mistakes
Managers Make
AND
How to Correct Them

THE 22 Biggest Mistakes Managers Make AND How to Correct Them

James K. Van Fleet

Parker Publishing Company, Inc.

West Nyack, N.Y.

© 1973 *by*

PARKER PUBLISHING COMPANY, INC.

West Nyack, N.Y.

Library of Congress Cataloging in Publication Data

Van Fleet, James K (date)
    The 22 biggest mistakes managers make and how to
correct them.

    Includes bibliographical references.
    1. Executives. 2. Management. 3. Personnel
management. I. Title.
HF5500.2.V35   658.4   72-10045
ISBN 0-13-935031-4

Printed in the United States of America

This book is dedicated to my wife
in token payment for her patience and understanding
while it was being written.

Other books by the author:

Guide to Managing People
How to Use the Dynamics of Motivation
Power with People
How to Put Yourself Across with People

What This Book Will Do for You

I used to think it was wrong to point out where a person might make a mistake, feeling that if he didn't know it could happen, then perhaps it wouldn't. I preferred always to use the positive approach.

But not long ago, in a seminar I was conducting, several young company executives and businessmen pointed out to me that this was like learning to drive a car, but not being taught what to do in case of an emergency. Or, they said, if one were inclined to water sports, it would be much like learning to sail a boat on a quiet lake, but not knowing what to do if a storm happened to come along.

"Isn't that why they hold lifeboat drill on those big ocean liners? Or why airlines brief you about what to do if there's a crash?" one man said.

"When I was taking business administration in college, I learned how a business operates under ideal conditions," another man said. "But I was never taught what to do when things went wrong. I've been with a company now for about eleven months and I've found that those perfect conditions my professor talked about don't even exist. I spend most of my time trying to solve problems I never heard of before or trying to set something right that someone else has messed up."

"He's right," still another man said. "I've run into the same thing. So why not give us the benefit of your experience? Tell us what to watch out for; tell us what to do when things go wrong. Or better yet, tell us what the worst mistakes are that we can make, and then give us some definite, concrete, positive measures we can use to correct these mistakes or learn how to avoid them."

I realized they were right. So with the help and advice from a lot of others—a shipping supervisor from Zenith, a production line foreman from General Electric, a college professor in economics from Drake, an office manager from the giant K-Mart system, a plant superintendent for Dayton Tire and Rubber, a store manager from Sears Roebuck, and many, many more—I wrote this book.

When you read it, you, too, will discover the twenty-two biggest mistakes managers make and how to correct them, or better yet, how to avoid making them. You'll come away with some definite, positive, and constructive ideas on how to get things done right the first time. Just for instance, you'll learn:

- How to keep abreast of developments in your own field,
- How to make sound and timely decisions,
- How to be prepared for advancement by assuming responsibility,
- How to inspect your department like an efficiency expert,
- How to make sure the job is understood, supervised, and accomplished,
- How to assess your own performance honestly and realistically,
- How to go for the maximum instead of accepting the minimum,
- How to develop a sense of responsibility in your subordinates,
- How to handle employee complaints like an expert counselor,
- How to criticize and make it sound like a compliment,
- How to bring out the best in your employees,

                                        . . . and much, much more.

James K. Van Fleet

Table of Contents

Do you give your boss problems or solutions? • **Do you** try to get all the facts first? • Do you use all available resources to get the job done? • Do you try to slough off the details? • Do you panic easily? • Are your reports based on actual results? • Do you meet deadlines? • Do you finish the job?

You won't have to accept the minimum • People will give their maximum efforts for you • Production and/or sales will go up • Costs and expenses will go down • This means increased profit, prestige, promotion for you

Set a high standard of performance for your organization • Don't accept the present system as the best or only way • Encourage your employees to better your system • Help people to set goals for themselves • Make a man proud of his job • Watch for these tell-tale signs of minimum performance

You can live with yourself • Your employees will trust you • You'll gain your employees' admiration and respect • You'll pull your employees up to your level

Use your managerial resources for their intended purposes • Practice the old-fashioned virtue of honesty • You must follow the rules, too • Give credit to your subordinates for the work they do • How to develop the character trait of unselfishness

People will believe what you say • You'll gain the reputation of being dependable • You'll be respected

When something goes wrong, do you tend to assume who's at fault? • Do you do your best to get all the facts first? • Do you make clear to the person his specific offense? • Do you control your temper when you're criticizing a person? • Do you always talk things over in private? • Do you praise before you criticize? • Do you share responsibility for the man's mistakes? • Do you listen to his side of the story, too? • Do you allow a person to retain his dignity? • Do you suggest specific steps to prevent reoccurrence of the mistake? • Do you keep accurate records? • Do you forgive and forget?

You'll Gain These Benefits by Paying Attention to Employee Complaints 184

You'll get to know and understand each employee better • Even though you're management, your employees will like you when you listen to them • Your people will know you're really interested in them • You'll find out what your employees really want when you listen to them

Techniques You Can Use to Gain These Benefits 185

Listening to problems is a manager's responsibility • How to be a good listener • How to turn an angry employee into a satisfied one just by listening • Twelve guidelines you can use to improve your handling of employee complaints

Benefits You Can Gain by Keeping Your People Informed 192

You'll encourage their initiative and enthusiasm • The well-informed employee is a better employee • You'll get rid of rumors • You'll gain a man's respect, obedience, cooperation, and support

Techniques You Can Use to Gain These Benefits 193

Let people know exactly where they stand with you • If you don't like a man's work, tell him so • If you do like a man's work, tell him that, too • How to praise a man properly • Tell him about company plans • Let your close assistants in on your plans at an early stage • How to eliminate misunderstandings • Let them know of any changes that will affect them • Let them know of any changes that will *not* affect them • Have your people tell you what *you have* to hear

ONE

Failing to Keep Abreast of
Developments in Your Own Field

Bob Horne was a bright young chemical engineer who once worked for the Reynolds Manufacturing Company in San Francisco. An MIT graduate, Bob was earmarked for early promotion and advancement. But he left the company in less than five years. Let me tell you what happened.

Bob used to spend about three hours a day getting from his suburban home in San Jose to his office and back again. As he drove to and from his work, he listened to the latest musical hits from the top forty on his stereo tape player.

Bob thought every now and then about taking some night courses at Stanford and doing some graduate work, but he never quite got around to it. He also gave some consideration to taking a correspondence course from the University, or, at the very least, subscribing to some of the best scientific journals in his field so he could keep up to date, but he seemed to be so tired from work and driving to and from the office every day that after a couple of drinks and dinner about all he could do was flop down in his favorite chair and watch television for an hour or so.

When the company offered to send him to Stanford at their expense so he could work on his master's degree, he asked them to postpone it for a couple of years as he was "simply worn out with going to school," he said. And when they sponsored a Dale Carnegie course for their junior executives and young management and supervisory personnel, again all at company expense, he declined because his wife was pregnant and needed him at home every night.

He'd often thought about joining the Bay Chapter of the Society of Professional Engineers. They met on Friday nights to discuss new developments in the field and to exchange ideas, but that was his poker night with the fellows in the neighborhood and he didn't want to miss that.

And what with Saturday morning on the golf course, doing some odd jobs around the house in the afternoon, driving into the city with Beth to see a movie, visit Chinatown, or have dinner at a good club on Saturday night, and then catching up on his sleep on Sunday, well, somehow Bob never did seem to be able to get around to doing anything at all about learning more than he'd known the day he got his sheepskin from MIT. So the company let him go. "Not qualified for further promotion," they said.

Now Jim Turner came to the company about the same time Bob did. Jim hadn't graduated from as prestigious a school as MIT. In fact, he got his engineering degree from a small midwestern college, Central Missouri State, in Warrensburg, Missouri.

Nor were his scholastic achievements as impressive as Bob's had been. Jim had only a 2.2 average on a 4-point scale, but he'd paid for 100 percent of his college expenses. He once worked as a bartender, which impressed the senior company recruiter, Andy Myers, who said, "Shows he knows how to talk with people and knows how to get along with them, too."

Jim also drove to and from work several hours a day. But he used his driving time to listen to pre-recorded tapes from Success Motivation Institute, a Waco, Texas, firm, the world's leading producer of personal motivation, supervision, leadership development, executive and management courses.

Of course, he did set some leisure time aside for golf, a movie now and then, or some other form of weekend entertainment for himself and his wife, but he budgeted his free time carefully for self-improvement.

Jim continued to work on his master's and took advantage of the company's offer to help him get it. He subscribed to the *Bureau of Business Practice* in Waterford, Connecticut, and became a member of two Prentice-Hall book clubs in Englewood Cliffs, New Jersey, the Business Leader's Book Club and the

Management Books Institute, so he could keep up to date on the latest ideas in the executive and management field.

All in all, Jim used every possible method he could think of to keep up on the latest developments in his own field. Today, just a little over eight years after he joined the company, Jim is the vice-president in charge of research and development. And he hasn't quit; he's still studying and working just as actively as ever to improve himself, not only in his own special profession of chemical engineering, but also, in the executive and management fields as well.

BENEFITS YOU'LL GAIN BY KEEPING ABREAST OF DEVELOPMENTS IN YOUR OWN FIELD

You'll Always Be Ready for Promotion

When you keep abreast of the latest developments in your own field, you'll always be ready for promotion at a moment's notice. And you must train yourself to be capable of taking over the next higher position at any time. If you're not ready . . . rest assured someone else will be.

You'll Always Be the Expert in Your Own Field

When you're the authority in your own line, people will look up to you. They'll admire you and respect you. They'll turn to you for advice and help. It'll be much easier for you to gain the obedience, cooperation, and full support of your subordinates. Your superiors will also respect your abilities and have confidence in you.

Your Job Will Be Interesting and Worthwhile

Of course, you'll gain material benefits when you keep abreast of the latest developments in your own field. But perhaps even more important—although I do have a healthy respect for money, too—you'll not wither away to stagnate and vegetate as you grow older. You can always keep your work new and interesting and exciting, and that in itself makes it well worthwhile.

Now to help you achieve these benefits and to keep you

from making the mistake Bob Horne made of failing to keep up with his chosen profession, let me tell you in more detail about some of the methods Jim Turner and many other successful managers and executives have used to become successful.

TECHNIQUES YOU CAN USE TO ACHIEVE THESE BENEFITS

Prepare Yourself for Advancement

"If you want to be considered for promotion up the corporate executive ladder, you must take the necessary action to prepare yourself for advancement," Jim says. "Without a doubt, the biggest obstacle to success for most people is the improper use of their leisure time. So your first big step is simply to learn how to *budget your time properly.*

"If you work 40 hours a week and sleep eight hours a night, you still have 72 hours a week left over. True enough, part of that time might still be considered as work hours, for you'll have to use some of them getting to your job and back home again, but even those driving hours don't have to be wasted.

"You can listen to pre-recorded tapes from SMI or some other company just as I do. Or while you're home, you can record certain data that you want to hear again, perhaps even commit to memory, and play those tapes on your recorder while you're driving to work."

My family physician, Doctor T. J. Burack, tells me he memorized every muscle in the body while riding a streetcar to George Washington University when he was attending medical school in St. Louis.

"Didn't have tape recorders in those days," Doc says. "At least not the kind you carry around with you or put in cars. So I'd type all the information about muscles on 3 by 5 cards. Name of the muscle would go on one side; its bony attachments, nerve and blood supply, and function would be on the other. I kept shuffling them from my left pocket to my right pocket as I memorized them. Used a lot of valuable time on those old streetcars while I was going to med school that otherwise would've been wasted looking out the window daydreaming or reading the comic strips and the sport page."

I realize you can't use every spare waking moment for

self-improvement, although some people seem to. Chet Atkins, for example, one of the finest guitar instrumentalists in the world, often carries his guitar to the table and keeps right on working on a new arrangement even while he's eating.

But you must leave some leisure moments for "fun and games" like golf, bowling, swimming, tennis, hand ball, or whatever it is you like to do. And keep some time open for your wife; do what she wants to do, too—at least part of the time. You should also reserve some time for those inevitable odd jobs around the house, mowing the lawn, going to the grocery store, getting the car fixed, and the like.

However, if you do budget your time carefully, I'm sure you'll find you still have about three hours four or five nights a week that you can use to good advantage instead of wasting it on television. Which leads me to this simple recommendation:

Stay away from the boob-tube! Television is a wonderful source of entertainment, but it can also turn you into a living vegetable if you allow it to do so. I usually watch the evening news. Once in a while a special catches my eye or an old movie stirs a nostalgic memory, but normally speaking, I'm settled down in my study with a book by seven o'clock in the evening, Monday through Thursday, four nights a week. I'm over fifty and I still feel I have a great deal to learn, and not nearly enough time left to do it in.

There's absolutely no substitute for knowledge. Lack of knowledge never has been and never will be an insurmountable obstacle to anyone, no matter how much or how little formal education a person has. Lack of knowledge is usually used more as an excuse than as a valid reason for not doing a job.

You can gain knowledge about any subject in the world if you have enough interest and desire to do so. You can ask questions, search for facts, pursue new ideas. Your age, your health, your job, even your financial status have no bearing at all on your ability to learn. If you want specific knowledge on any given subject, *look for it—find it—learn it.*

You can gain information and facts about anything simply by developing the public library habit. By being selective in your reading, you can become a private student and have the greatest teachers in the world right there at your fingertips. Or you can take advantage of your state university's extension courses. Enrollment and study in a correspondence course can make you the master of whatever subject you choose.

Accept Managerial Training When It's Offered to You

At first glance, this would seem like an unnecessary recommendation, but George Bancroft, Director of Management Training for Amber Industries of Paterson, New Jersey, tells me that it isn't.

"Our company really goes all out to get our executives their college degree," Mr. Bancroft says. "For instance, Columbia University has an adult education course called Master's Degree for Executives, although you don't need a bachelor's degree to enroll. However, several years of middle or top-level administrative experience are a must.

"The sponsoring company must certify that the applicant is headed for higher level responsibilities. We also have to pay a $7,500 fee for the course. The individual himself must pass a standard admissions test for graduate study in business.

"The course itself consists of classes one day a week, three full week sessions each quarter, and 15 hours of homework a week. The studies last for two years and upon successful completion of the course a Master's Degree is awarded.

"Now wouldn't you think people would jump at a chance like that? Well, amazingly, they don't. They give a variety of reasons for not being able to go, but in the final analysis, the most prevalent one of all is the loss of free time because of the 15 hours of homework every week!"

Don't Under-Rate Technical Skills

No question about it, management is an art, but its most successful practitioners have always had a solid foundation of competence in the less glamorous and more tedious techniques of business administration.

And no matter what your own professional specialty is—planning, organization, budgeting, quality control, research and development, statistical analysis, problem-solving, general economics—all of the subjects in the regular curriculum of business education are valuable tools to the manager and the executive at every level.

So if you do happen to be weak in any one of these—or in any other area I've not mentioned, but that is specifically needed for your own particular kind of work—then bone up by going to night school, taking a correspondence course, or simply by reading at home.

Expose Yourself to New Ideas

You should train yourself to be receptive to new ideas, no matter how revolutionary they might seem to you at first. Even if these new ideas do upset some of your most cherished beliefs, you must be realistic enough to recognize an improvement when you see one.

New ideas are the very basis and foundation of personal and professional growth. They challenge you; they open up new horizons to explore; they help keep your imagination scrubbed up and sparkling. And from a practical viewpoint, new ideas can many times help you solve a lot of your problems, both old and new.

"Executives and managers who get things done almost always are those who are the most curious about new ideas," says Gordon Hawkins, President of the Iowa State Board of Realtors. "First of all, they don't think it's beneath their dignity to learn from other people—even their own subordinates. Nor are they afraid to expose their ignorance about specific areas in front of someone who can help them learn something worth while."

If you do want to expose yourself to new ideas and new viewpoints so you can keep up with things, then follow these four simple guidelines:

1. Read some less familiar newspapers, magazines, and books.
2. Talk to new people, both within and outside your company.
3. Go to unfamiliar places once in a while. Expose yourself to new customs, new impressions, new experiences.
4. Do anything at all that will shake up the way you currently think, act, talk, read, look at things. It's a tonic for apathy and lethargy.

Really Look for Ways to Improve Yourself

When you get right down to bare-bone facts, it's up to you to teach yourself management skills and to continue to grow and keep up with developments in your own field. So whether your firm has an executive training program or not, your own career growth is entirely up to you. Here are a couple of key points you can follow and use to do that:

Reach out for more responsibility. You start to grow when your job is just a little too big for you to handle easily without effort. If your present duties are no longer a real challenge to you, then it's time for you to look around—*especially above you*—for new fields of conquest.

For instance, tell your boss you'd like to relieve him of some of his routine daily problems so he can have more time for high level policy decisions. Of course, you're not going to fool him. He knows you're looking for more responsibility. After all, he came up the same way himself. And you can bet he'll reward you with more work, too.

Be your own taskmaster. Management experts learned a long time ago that no one can train an executive or a manager in the same way you teach a person to be a typist or a file clerk or a secretary. Executive development is primarily self-development even though your company might go all out to provide ideal conditions to help you grow.

This is important to remember because many young executives think managerial skills can be learned only in a college course or at a management institute.

But to tell the truth, what you learn on the job and through well-planned homework becomes even more important because it teaches you self-development through *practical application* of what you've learned in school. We all learn best by doing, whether it's swimming, riding a bicycle, throwing a ball, playing a piano, or executive management.

Let Yourself Grow on the Job

Dennis Allen is a personnel recruiter for Delco-Remy, a division of General Motors. He knows his work, enjoys it, and does it well, for of the men he has selected during his years with the company, 17 have risen to the rank of corporate vice-president in GM and one has become president.

"When a young man starts to work for us as a junior executive, he finds his duties are more administrative than managerial," Mr. Allen says. "But as he moves on up through successively higher levels of management, he will find that the nature of his work undergoes a gradual change. At the lowest level of management, he is supervising only one particular kind of work. At the next level, he will have charge of an entire process that will probably involve the integration of several different skills.

"Finally, if he does reach the very top, he finds he has to be increasingly concerned with the philosophy of management. Today, our chief executives must look far ahead into the future and far beyond the immediate problems of Delco-Remy and General Motors to clearly define the long-range objectives of the corporation.

"Management on this level demands a sense of social responsibility. It is no job at all for a man whose cultural horizons are limited by market reports, sales charts, and production figures. Top management today has to be as concerned with pollution of the environment as it is with profits for the stockholder, if, in fact, not more so."

So there you have some of the methods you can use to keep abreast of new developments in your own field. Use them; they'll help you. But don't stop there. Develop some of your own techniques, too; you'll be an even better manager when you do.

TWO

Confining Yourself to Your Own Specialty

John Kelly and Ralph Reynolds are both under consideration for promotion to the position of production superintendent in the Springdale plant of the Dayton Rubber and Tire Company. The final decision of selection is up to George Orr, the plant manager.

Both men are qualified, not only by education, but also by experience on the job. Each one is a department foreman. Kelly is a good administrator; his office records are meticulous. His production figures are high. He competes vigorously with other departments and hates to accept defeat. On paper, he has a slight edge over his competitor in his specialty, both in production and administration. He is somewhat weak, though, in his understanding of other departments in the plant and his appreciation of company problems as a whole.

When asked what his career goal was, he said, "To be the best department foreman in the plant." And as George Orr says, "He is!"

Now Ralph Reynolds is perhaps not quite as good an administrator as Kelly. He admits he hates to be confined to his office doing paperwork. His production meets plant standards and requirements, both in quality and quantity. He knows how to work with other departments; he cooperates with people. He makes every effort to identify company goals and objectives with his own. Ralph also tries to expand his knowledge of the entire plant by spending some of his off-duty hours visiting other departments so he can better understand their problems and how they function.

When asked what his career goal was, he said, "To be the company president."

With these facts in mind, which man would you select for promotion? John Kelly or Ralph Reynolds? I would pick Ralph Reynolds. In fact, so did George Orr. Here are his reasons why:

"John Kelly is the best department foreman in the plant because that's exactly what he wants to be," says George. "That's fortunate for us, perhaps, for we do need good department foremen, but unfortunate for John. By taking such a narrow approach to his career and by confining himself only to his own field, he has limited his opportunity for promotion.

"On the other hand, Ralph Reynolds has shown us that his career objective is much higher. He wants to be the company president and he knows he can't begin to achieve that goal unless he knows everything there is to know about every department in the company. Personally, I think he'll make it clear to the top and I hope he does."

The point is that if you confine yourself only to your own specialized field, chances are you'll become little more than a skilled technician, and that's not what you want. You want to be a manager—an executive. Before I take up some specific techniques you can use to keep from making the same mistake John Kelly made, let me first tell you about some . . .

BENEFITS YOU'LL GAIN BY NOT CONFINING YOURSELF ONLY TO YOUR OWN SPECIALTY

You'll Have Better Opportunity for Higher Promotion

Confining yourself to your own specialty might possibly bring you faster promotion in the beginning, but your advancement will be limited. Corporations and companies are so complex and so diversified in their operations today that to reach the top you must diversify, too. Don't limit your knowledge and your chance for promotion by over-specializing.

The Higher You Go, the Better the Financial Return

What it really boils down to here is that the greater your responsibility, the greater will be your material benefits and your financial return. And the more capable you become in your ability to manage a diversity of complex and intricate operations, the more responsibility you will be given, the higher you'll go, the more salary you'll command.

Your Career Will Be Much More Interesting

Frankly, I cannot visualize doing one job for 30 or 40 years. Yet I know people who've done and are still doing exactly that. Most of them are sick of the rut they're in. They hang on until retirement age simply because they have no other choice. So if you're interested in keeping your job exciting and worthwhile, don't overspecialize; diversify and expand your capabilities. Your job will be much more interesting when you do. In fact, when you do this, your work is no longer just a job; it becomes a career.

TECHNIQUES YOU CAN USE TO GAIN THE BENEFITS

Set Your Goals High

Paul J. Meyer, President of Success Motivation Institute, has come up with an excellent formula for setting your goals high and motivating yourself to reach them. An expert in inspiring managers, executives and supervisors to give their utmost, Mr. Meyer calls this formula his . . .

MILLION DOLLAR PERSONAL SUCCESS PLAN *

Crystallize your thinking. Determine what specific goal you want to achieve and establish a time limit for its achievement.

Develop a plan for achieving your goal. Establish a deadline for its attainment. Plan your progress carefully —hour by hour, day by day, month by month.

Develop a sincere desire for the things you want. A burning desire is the greatest motivator of every human action.

Develop supreme confidence in yourself and your own abilities. Enter every activity without giving mental recognition to the possibility of defeat.

---

* Reprinted by permission of Paul J. Meyer, President of Success Motivation Institute, Inc., of Waco, Texas. All rights reserved. Copyright 1962.

Develop a dogged determination to follow through on your plan, regardless of the obstacles, criticism, or circumstances that you might encounter.

Now let's discuss Mr. Meyer's Million Dollar Personal Success Plan in more detail so we can expand and amplify his ideas.

Crystallize your thinking. To do this, you must be specific about what you want. Focus down sharply on your desires, your goals, your ambitions.

You cannot be vague. Generalities like *wealthy by middle-age . . . retire when I make enough to live comfortably . . .* these are not enough. You should establish a definite goal. If it's money you want, you should specify the exact amount you want to have by a certain date. Give yourself a realistic figure and a reasonable deadline.

Or perhaps the attainment of a certain position in a company is what you're after. Whatever your goal might be, dedicate all your energies to its achievement. Don't let yourself be distracted by any person or any event. Know exactly what you want, where you want to go, and when you want to get there.

Develop a plan for achieving your goal. You'll be amazed at how quickly this will change your fanciful daydreams into definite concrete desires. So write down your plan. Say in black and white what it is that you want to attain.

Break up your plan into an outline form with intermediate steps and checkpoints. Then you can see how you're getting along. Always let your steps overlap; that is to say, never check one step off as being done until you've started to work on the next one. This will keep you from stopping short of your final goal.

Develop a sincere desire for the things you want. What is it you expect to receive when you reach your goal? A bigger house, a new car, a cottage on the lake, material success? Make a complete list of every benefit you can think of that you'll receive when you reach your goal. Don't stop at financial benefits and material successes only. List how you'll benefit in other ways, too: improvement of your personality, your ability to get along with people, for example. These are worthwhile goals to be added to your list, too.

Develop supreme confidence in yourself and your own abilities. For this, you should concentrate on your strengths instead of your weaknesses. Maintain a firm faith in yourself and your abilities to accomplish your purposes, no matter what your limitations might be. The history books are full of names of famous people who overcame tremendous obstacles to achieve their goals and become successful.

Make a study of some of these people. Note especially the handicaps. List the weak points they had and chances are you'll find you don't have as many disadvantages to overcome as they had. So if they could succeed, then why can't you? You can if you'll just have confidence in yourself and in your own abilities to do the job.

Follow through on your plan with determination and perseverance. The obstacle doesn't exist that cannot be overcome if you have enough desire, determination, and perseverance to stick to your plan no matter what happens. Make your determination to succeed so strong that it will eliminate any situation or circumstance that stands in your way. Persevere to the end and it's impossible for anyone or anything to stop you.

Don't Limit Your Knowledge to Your Own Specialty

"All managers and executives ought to recognize that they must have a lifetime of schooling to stay on top today," says Robert Van Horn, President of Van Horn and Associates, a management consulting firm in Seattle, Washington. "Each man should have his own self-improvement, self-education program. This should include wide reading about what is going on, not only in his own, but also in other fields as well. He can also use correspondence schools and extension courses for continual self-improvement."

A little later on I'll take up some of the techniques you can use right in your own company to gain knowledge about fields other than your own, but right here I'd like to tell you how valuable I've found college level adult education courses to be.

I've taken a variety of both credit and non-credit courses in college, ranging from sociology and economics to salesmanship and marketing. I've absorbed courses in psychology and philosophy. I've usually studied subjects that interested me since I wasn't working toward any degree.

One time I took a course in salesmanship and I was surprised to find that the fellow sitting next to me was a buyer for a chain of midwestern department stores.

"I don't understand why you're taking a course in salesmanship when you're a buyer," I said. "You don't have to sell anyone anything."

"Oh, it's really not too surprising," he said. "I thought if I could understand the principles of salesmanship better and study the art of selling from the salesman's point of view, then I'd be in a far better position to buy logically and sensibly for my company. When I understand how a salesman sells and the arguments he uses, then I can keep from making emotional decisions and snap judgments when I buy."

Good point, of course. A lot of business organizations today feel the same way about adult education. A great many companies feel their employees should expand their learning in fields other than their own specialty. So they offer opportunities to their management personnel to continue their education in a wide variety of stimulating business-oriented courses.

General Electric, for instance, has more than 400 technical courses for their engineers. They also offer those same engineers innumerable courses in accounting, marketing, public speaking, public relations, and the like, so they can expand their knowledge and their know-how far beyond their own specialty.

The Amway Corporation of Ada, Michigan—one of the biggest and most successful direct sales companies in the world (they're in Canada and Australia as well as the United States)— has established a leadership development training program to help their more than 150,000 distributors improve themselves.

Their review board screens hundreds of business and professional self-improvement books to see if they are appropriate for the high standards of the Amway leadership development training program. Representative titles they've selected include *The Magic of Thinking Big* by David Schwartz, *How I Raised Myself from Failure to Success in Selling* by Frank Bettger, *How to Have Confidence and Power in Dealing with People* by Les Giblin. All three of these are published by Prentice-Hall, Englewood Cliffs, New Jersey. One of my own books, *Power with People,** has also been chosen by them for use in their leadership development courses.

"The Amway system of reviewing, selecting, and recom-

---

* James K. Van Fleet, *Power with People* (West Nyack, New York; Parker Publishing Company, 1970).

mending self-improvement books for their distributors to study is especially helpful to me," says Charlie Miller, one of their distributors from Ames, Iowa. "First of all, I trust their judgment; they're experts. Secondly, I just don't have time to read hundreds of books to pick out the best ones. Time is money to me."

For companies that cannot or do not want to sponsor special courses themselves, the tuition refund plan is both a popular and a practical way of encouraging executives to go on with their schooling. Under this plan, the company pays part of the tuition of any employee who takes an improved business or business-oriented course outside the company.

"Although we have our own company training program at various levels, we've found this added approach to education very useful," says Henry Goetz, vice president in charge of Midwestern Life Insurance Company's personnel division. "And we're not too inflexible when it comes to deciding what a business course is. If a man wants to improve his education, we'll bend over backward to help him. If he feels that a certain course will improve his personal or professional qualifications, we'll pay for it."

So check with your own company to see what their policy is about furthering your education. Maybe you've been missing the boat all along. And if they don't have such a policy, maybe you can get them to start one by sending you to school. If neither one of these works, then it's all up to you to go it on your own, just as I have done.

Learn Everything There Is to Know About Your Company

Do you want to be president of your company some day? Then learn everything there is to know about every department in the plant: what they do, what their exact duties are, what special problems they have.

Spend an extra hour a day in the plant. Come in an hour early or stay over for an hour after you're through work. But don't spend it in your own department or just sitting around shooting the breeze. Spend that hour in another section of the plant—shipping, production, budgeting, quality control, engineering, the warehouse, reclamation and salvage.

"That's how I learned every department here in Springdale," Ralph Reynolds says. "To tell the truth, that's what helped me become production superintendent. I simply knew more about every single department in the plant than anyone else.

"Oh, I don't mean I know more than Bill Henry does about the V-Belt Department—after all, he's foreman over there; but I do know more about research and development, shipping, the warehouse, and so on, then Bill does. And the same goes for the other foremen in the plant, too. Not that I'm any smarter than they are; I'm not. My extra knowledge came from looking and watching and asking questions all the time."

Learn Something New Each Day About Someone Else's Job

Once you've got the picture of your company well in mind by learning the functions and the problems of every department, then start learning the details of every job in the place.

Oh, I'm sure you're not going to remember the intricate details of every man's job forever—that's impossible; but you'll know his job well enough to be able to talk about it intelligently. Not only that, no one'll ever be able to pull your leg about what the duties of a certain job are, or how difficult it is to do. You'll know for sure yourself and you'll have that valuable information from first-hand knowledge.

"I've watched the detailed work of every job in this place," says Sam Freeman, night foreman at Lily Tulip's plant in Springfield, Missouri. "I've never been backward about exposing my ignorance to any employee by asking him questions about his work.

"I've always found that when he knows I'm sincere, he'll do everything he can to fill me in on his job. Today, although I might not be able to do his job specifically or as well as he does, I can tell immediately when he's doing something wrong, and that's important to any supervisor in production to know."

Look Beyond Your Own Company

You can do this in many ways. First of all, you can widen your interests and broaden your knowledge by joining outside organizations. And whether it be in civic or professional activities, the community will come to know you as a concerned responsible person who works for the XYZ Company. This association will certainly do both you and your firm a lot of good.

Another excellent method is used by Jack Lowrey, Personnel Manager for Cummins Diesel in Kansas City, Missouri.

"I make it a point to visit a non-competitive company at least one day a month," Jack says. "And we extend invitations to others to see our plant and our method of operation, too.

"I've visited many of our customers and our suppliers this way. And we've taken them on tours of our place. The mutual exchange of information has proven extremely beneficial to all of us and it helps us understand the other person's problems. In my own individual case, it gives me a wonderful opportunity to exchange ideas and pick up new information on personnel management procedures."

You'll discover other ways to keep from confining yourself to your own specialty, I'm sure. Add them to the ones you've learned here and use them all. You'll be sure to benefit when you do.

THREE

Refusing to Seek Higher Responsibility or Take Responsibility for Your Actions

Although you must possess a great many outstanding leadership traits to qualify you for a top-level position in the executive management field, there is one capability above all that you must have, or you'll never make it. That is your willingness to look for additional *higher* responsibility and to take complete responsibility for your own actions.

As a manager or an executive in a company, a plant, a store, a division, or a department, you will no doubt be given the full power to decide upon a course of action—to give orders—to guide and correct the actions of others.

And as that manager or executive, you must be willing to assume full responsibility for your own individual actions or for your failure to take action. You should also be willing to assume the full responsibility for all your organization does or fails to do—for its failures as well as for its successes.

To you, then, will go either the glory or the blame. If it's glory, you must be prompt to pass the credit and the commendations on down to others. But you must accept the blame yourself.

Of course, you'll be expected to take the proper corrective action to remedy a bad situation, but you cannot pass the buck. You, and you alone, have to accept full responsibility for the mistakes of your subordinates. As an executive or a manager, you cannot get by with saying, "But I told him to do it this way. It's not my fault that he didn't." This will never be accepted as an explanation for failure; it will be regarded only as an excuse.

For instance, at Gettysburg after Pickett's courageous but futile charge against the center of the Union lines ended in defeat and disaster for the Confederate forces, a young Southern officer came up to General Lee and tried to console him.

"It was not your fault, General Lee," he said. "In all truth, the inexcusable acts of others made failure inevitable."

But General Lee refused to blame others for the defeat of his forces. He answered the young officer in the way every responsible leader must answer when he said, "No, that is not true; it was all my fault."

You would be extremely wise to follow General Lee's example yourself. Don't try to evade the responsibility for failure by passing the buck to someone else. If you do that, your superiors will see through your flimsy facade at once, and you'll be very likely to lose your position of confidence and trust.

So instead of trying to avoid the blame, accept the full responsibility. When you do, you'll discover certain . . .

BENEFITS YOU'LL GAIN BY SEEKING A HIGHER RESPONSIBILITY AND BY ACCEPTING FULL RESPONSIBILITY FOR YOUR OWN ACTIONS

You'll Learn to Assume the Initiative

When you look for increased responsibilities, you'll learn to take the initiative. You'll not wait for your company or your boss to tell you what you ought to do. You'll be doing it while they're still thinking about it. You'll have the solution before they've discovered the problem.

When your subordinates know you are willing to step forward and take the initiative—when they know you are actively looking for higher responsibilities—and when they know you will take full responsibility for your own actions—they'll gain confidence in you and they'll trust your decisions and your orders. And so will your superiors.

You'll Increase Your Professional Stature

When you look for additional higher responsibilities—and when you are willing to assume complete responsibility for your own actions—you'll develop yourself professionally; you'll increase your management and executive abilities.

So make it a point to accept every bit of responsibility you can handle—and then some. Look for it; accept it eagerly. One of the fastest and surest ways to climb the executive and management ladder is to make yourself known. And you can do that by volunteering for the really tough jobs.

When you complete that tough assignment successfully, you'll increase your confidence in yourself and in your own abilities to get the job done. Your boss will have greater confidence in you, too. And so will your subordinates.

You'll Gain the Respect and Confidence of Your Superiors

Employers always respect a person who has the courage to take a calculated risk, make a sound decision, and then accept full responsibility for his actions. They know that if you won't take a chance—if you won't stick your neck out once in a while—you don't have what it takes for a top management job.

At the same time, your boss will have no use for you if you try to pass the buck when you do make a mistake. Even when you're wrong, even when you've failed, your boss will still have respect for you and confidence in you if you will accept the full responsibility for failure.

You'll Have the Obedience, Cooperation, and Support of Your Subordinates

When your subordinates realize that you'll assume responsibility, not only for your own actions, *but also for theirs,* you'll gain their willing obedience, their full cooperation, and their loyal support. You'll be able to get them to do exactly as you want them to do. But if you fail to accept this responsibility, you'll lose completely the confidence and the backing of your own subordinates.

When You Look for Responsibility—It Will Find You

Look for responsibility and it will always find you. Whenever leaders look for responsibility, somehow it always finds them. You cannot become a successful manager, a top-flight executive, an outstanding leader in your chosen field unless you really look for the opportunity for bigger and higher responsibilities. Waiting for responsibility to come your way is never enough. You must get out and find it.

TECHNIQUES YOU CAN USE TO ACHIEVE THE BENEFITS

Know Your Cardinal Responsibilities

"If you're going to accept full responsibility for what you do, then you must know what your cardinal responsibilities are so you can concentrate on them," says Roger Sanderson, manager of one of the branch stores of the giant K-Mart chain in Kansas City, Missouri.

"This means you must be able to tell the difference between what you alone *must do* and what your subordinates *can do*. Once you know specifically what the exact duties of your job are, then you're in a much better position to carry them out. But no one wants a job where the responsibilities and the duties are vague and ill-defined. This can lead to nothing but confusion and frustration."

Now when you follow Mr. Sanderson's advice, you'll be able to concentrate on the essential points: the basic fundamentals. You'll be able to fulfill the cardinal responsibilities of your own job. When you do that, you'll not be tempted to meddle and become involved in the details of a subordinate's job. Stick to your own problems and solve them; that should keep you quite busy enough.

Do Every Job to the Best of Your Ability

"If you want to be rewarded by increased opportunity to perform bigger and more important tasks, then you ought to perform every assigned job to the best of your ability," says Melvin W. Peterson, the chief inspector in charge of Union Carbide's quality control division in their Pittsburgh plant. "If you can't be trusted to do the small and tedious jobs well, your boss will never see fit to trust you with a greater responsibility.

"I don't care whether your job is big or little, exciting or dull, important or seemingly not worth while to you. There's an old cliché that seems to fit the situation here and sums up my idea quite well, I think. That is, *anything worth doing at all is worth doing well.*

"I realize that here in the quality control division we might emphasize this point more than in other departments, but we have to. Every time one of our products is returned by a customer because it's defective, someone in this division's to blame. Someone failed to do the best job he could."

I agree with Mr. Peterson. Do every assigned task to the best of your ability, no matter what it is. If you don't agree with this concept, then something really ought to be changed. In other words, if you happen to think that the particular job you're doing isn't worth while and really isn't worth doing well, then maybe it isn't and it ought to be eliminated.

If you really do feel that way about it, then tell your boss. But if you're not willing to do that, then do that distasteful job to the best of your ability. You really have no other choice if you're going to take full responsibility for your actions.

Have the Courage of Your Convictions

"Do what you know is right and stick to it," says Phil Curtis, one of the founders and co-owner of Curtis and Williams Advertising and Public Relations in Phoenix, Arizona. "Say what you know is true and stick to your guns. Have the courage of your inner convictions. It's hard to live with yourself if you don't.

"Anybody can say yes; that's easy. That's why yes-men are always a dime a dozen in any organization; they're a glut on the market. But the man who has the courage to say 'No' or the guts to tell his boss he's wrong is a rarity. He may not be liked at times, but you can bet one thing for sure: He's respected by everyone for not being a yes-man.

"One of our copywriters is like that, thank God. Pete's been with us for years and he never pulls punches. My partner or I might come up with what we think is a tremendous idea. Everybody around here agrees with us; afraid not to, I guess.

"But then we ask Pete. I don't know how often he's said, 'No damned good!' in the last 20 years, but I know he's saved Al and me from making complete fools of ourselves many, many times!"

And you, too, have the responsibility to *tell your boss*

what he has to hear—not what he wants to hear—especially when he asks for your honest opinion. If you can't do that, you're simply not worth the salary he's paying you. Oh, I know it's tough to do that with some bosses, but to tell the truth, if you can't, then wouldn't you be better off somewhere else?

Assume Responsibility for the Failures of Your Subordinates

What it really comes down to here is determining what your own responsibility is first of all. If you're being paid to see that the job is done, then you'll have to assume the responsibility for failure when it isn't.

Now I'll admit at once that it's easy to take the credit—but tough to take the blame when you make a mistake. But when your boss criticizes you, not only for your own failures but also for the failures of those who work for you, that's doubly hard to take. You'll need both character and courage to absorb the blame for the mistakes of others. But that's one of the occupational hazards of being a manager; it goes with the job.

Assume Full Responsibility for Your Own Actions

"There are several simple guidelines you can use to teach yourself how to assume full responsibility for your own actions," says Earl Young, West Coast Sales Manager for Colony Paints. "Nothing complicated about them. First of all:

"**You must be decisive.**   Be willing to assume the responsibility for your assessment of the facts and your estimate of the situation in any given set of circumstances. Do that and you'll motivate your own subordinates to be confident and decisive and to assume responsibility, too.

"**When you goof—admit it.**   When you make a mistake don't try to rationalize away your errors, look for a scapegoat, or go off and sit in a corner and sulk. None of your subordinates expect you to be infallible, so you won't lose face when you admit you're wrong. When you do make a mistake and admit it, your subordinates will gain confidence in your fairness and honesty, an asset that is beyond price to any manager or executive.

"**Accept criticism gracefully.** This can be hard to do if you've got a thin skin. If criticism bothers you, ask yourself these three questions:

> *Who* is criticizing me?
> *What* are his qualifications?
> *Why* is he criticizing me?

"Questions like these will help you judge the validity of your critic's comments and the motives behind them. After you've heard him out, weigh his remarks. Were they really true? Did you have it coming? Did he have all the facts? Was he generalizing? If what he said makes sense, accept his criticism willingly and gracefully, correct the mistakes he's brought to your attention, and be thankful he did so."

These are good points to remember that Mr. Young brought out. I'd like to add only one thought to his and that is:

You are also responsible for what you fail to do. One of the common mistakes young managers and executives (and a lot of old ones, too) make is not to realize that they're also as responsible for what they *didn't do* as they are for what they *did do*.

In other words, the mistakes of *omission* will often outweigh the mistakes of *commission*. Assumption of individual responsibility covers not only what you do, but also what you fail to do. Or as an old preacher friend of mine puts it: "Just being good will never get you into Heaven; you've got to be good for something."

Ask for Diversified Management Assignments

When I was in the army many years ago I learned that if I wanted to be assigned to a certain job or a specific post, I'd never get what I wanted unless I asked for it.

One summer I was stationed at Fort Leonard Wood, Missouri. My family and I were in old World War II wooden barracks that had been converted into temporary family quarters. The evenings were getting chilly in the fall so I decided to look for the heating plant.

To my dismay, I discovered an old coal furnace in the

outside utility room. "Do you know how to stoke a coal furnace?" I asked my wife. "No," she replied. "Neither do I," I said. "We'd better get out of here before winter comes."

The next morning I read a squib in the Post Daily Bulletin to the effect that qualified officers interested in studying a foreign language at the Army Language School in Monterey, California, should submit written applications for consideration. Openings were especially plentiful in the Chinese Mandarin language.

Well, I didn't waste any time submitting a written application through channels. I figured letters took too long and had to go through too many headquarters for approval. Besides, I'd had experience with that system before. I didn't want my application lying forgotten in some clerk's in-basket somewhere. Winter was too close for that!

So that afternoon I called Officer Career Management in the Pentagon. I convinced them that I was the most promising officer they had around to study Chinese Mandarin, in spite of the fact that I'd flunked both French and Spanish in college! Less than sixty days later we were comfortably settled down in new quarters on the beautiful and charming Monterey Peninsula overlooking the blue Pacific, safe and sound far away from the blizzards of the midwest. And all because I made my desires known *first* to the right people.

Corporation top management reacts the same way. The squeaking wheel always gets the grease. W. R. Nelson, a top executive with Chrysler Corporation, puts it this way: "We expect our young executives to be highly vocal—to speak up. If they want more responsibility, they should go to their bosses and ask for it—and, if necessary, they should fight for it.

"We do all we can to encourage people to reach out for wider experience and more authority. But we can't read their minds. When a young executive asks for more responsibility, we know he wants it, and he'll get it. If he can handle it, fine. If he can't, the sooner he finds out, the better for both of us."

These, then, are some of the techniques you can use to reach out for higher responsibility. There are two more I'd like to mention here even though we don't have the time for a full discussion of them. They are quite self-explanatory, though, and I know that you'll be able to apply them yourself without any further explanation or help from me.

1. Know every facet of your superior's job. Learn his duties completely and thoroughly. Be prepared to take over his job and his responsibilities at a moment's notice.
2. In the absence of instructions, be prepared to seize the initiative. Take the action you feel your superior would tell you to take if he were present.

FOUR

Failure to Make Sound and Timely Decisions

Your ability to make a decision will depend, of course, to a large part on how much authority your superiors have granted you. The question is: Will you actually use the authority you've been given to make decisions, or will you be paralyzed into helpless inactivity by the fear of making a mistake?

Before you answer that question, please listen to what Mr. Lloyd L. Lambert, a top-level executive with Republic Industrial Tool Corporation, has to say about executive and management decision making.

"Other than financial gain, one of the primary reasons an executive or manager hungers for promotion is that the higher the position, the more power he'll have to make bigger and more important decisions without undue outside interference. That higher position will give him the power he needs to get things done," Mr. Lambert says.

"But then amazingly, when he does get the power he wants, his attitude changes completely and he often hesitates to use it. This reluctance shows up in his hesitation to make decisions. He hems and haws—fiddles and procrastinates—appoints a committee to study the problem—waits for further developments in the situation, in fact, he will go far out of his way to avoid making a decision of any kind that could be traced back to him.

"The executive suites of hundreds of companies and corporations are overloaded with so-called managers and executives who are deathly afraid to make decisions about anything more important than the time of the morning and afternoon coffee breaks, or when to let the secretary take her lunch period!"

If you want to avoid joining that crowd, you must develop your ability to make sound and timely decisions. You must become adept at isolating the heart of a problem. You will need several capacities to do this.

First of all, you will need judgment so that after considering all the factors bearing on the problem and all the ways of solving it, you will be able to determine the best workable solution. Your logic and reasoning must also be sound if you're going to attain that good judgment you need. And you must be farsighted enough to anticipate and plan for all the actions and reactions that will come from your decision.

"What will happen if . . . ?" must always be the question in the back of your mind as you look over all the possible solutions to your problem so you can make a wise decision. You must be able to identify the important things and have the knack of taking care of first things first.

And there is at least one more important capacity you'll need. You must possess the strength of character it takes to make decisions at the proper time and to announce them at the right time and place so you can gain the desired results.

BENEFITS YOU'LL GAIN BY MAKING SOUND AND TIMELY DECISIONS

People Will Have Confidence in You As a Leader

Both your superiors and your subordinates will have confidence in your abilities as a leader when you show them that you are able to make a rapid and accurate estimate of the situation, as well as being capable of reaching a sound and timely decision. To make that sound and timely decision, you'll need to gather together all the facts—to analyze and sift them—to make up your mind—and then to issue your order with complete confidence that you've done the right thing.

People Will Trust Your Decisions and Your Orders

If you're able to reason logically and reach your decision quickly as to what course of action you're going to take, no matter what the situation, people will trust your orders. They'll have confidence in you and they'll be impressed by your good judgment. And they'll want to do their best for you, too.

You'll Become Known As an Expert Trouble-Shooter

When circumstances come up that cause you to make a change in your plans or that require a new decision or a different procedure, prompt and positive action on your part will build people's confidence and trust in you. You'll become known as an expert in problem solving and in getting things done. You'll be known as a person who makes things happen. Such a reputation will definitely enhance your stature in the organization.

You'll Rid Yourself of Frustration

The inability to make up your mind is a leading source of frustration, not only in business and management, but also in solving the personal problems in your life. When you use the scientific methods of problem solving and decision making that you'll learn in this chapter, you'll rid yourself of that frustration. You'll have confidence in yourself and your own abilities to deal with pressure. And that's more than half the battle.

TECHNIQUES YOU CAN USE TO GAIN THESE BENEFITS

Do Your Worrying Before You Place Your Bet

A great many people make decisions on spur-of-the-moment impulses and then spend the rest of their time worrying about the outcome of those decisions. I used to do the same thing myself until I learned differently from Doctor Leon Utterback, a Los Angeles psychiatrist.

"Do your worrying before you place your bet, not after the dice are thrown," Dr. Utterback says. "I learned that during a vacation trip I made to Las Vegas in 1968. I'd decided to try my luck at one of the crap games in the Golden Nugget, but before long I became more interested in the people around the table than I was in the game.

"I noticed person after person who seemed not to worry at

all before the dice were cast. They would bet impulsively as if following some inner hunch. They paid no attention whatever to the odds involved. But then the moment the dice were thrown, they froze up and began to worry whether the shooter would make his point or not.

"How foolish people are, I thought. If they're going to worry or be concerned or figure the odds, the time to do all that is before they place their bet—not afterward. There's something they can do about it then. If a man wants to gamble, then he ought to figure out the best odds possible or decide not to take the risk at all. But after the bets are down and after the dice are thrown, you might as well forget it. There's not one thing you can do then to change or influence the outcome."

Dr. Utterback's theory is actually even more applicable to the process of decision making in business and management than it is to gambling. The point is, though, that a great many people do make business decisions just about the same way those Las Vegas tourists do. They make up their minds hastily without thinking about the consequences. They embark on courses of action without adequate preparation, without considering all the risks involved, and without figuring out the best alternatives.

The best way to make a decision, as Dr. Utterback says, is to *do your worrying before you place your bet.* In other words, do everything you can do first to make sure the right decision is made. But once you've made that decision and execution is the order of the day, then stop worrying and fretting about the outcome.

The rest of this chapter will be spent in showing you how to do just that. You can get off to the right start if you will . . .

Ask Yourself These Five Questions First

1. Do *I* have to make this decision?

Is this really your decision to make or does it belong to someone else? Here you must know the boundaries and the limits of your own job. You must know which decisions you and you alone *must* make, and which decisions your subordinates *can* make.

Don't interfere with your people's work. Let them carry

out the details of their own job. If you do decide that no one else but you can make this decision, then prepare yourself properly so you can make the right one. But if it belongs to someone else, then get rid of it. Unload it as you would a hot potato. Give the problem to the right man to solve. That in itself is a wise decision.

2. *What* do I have to decide?

In other words, is there really a problem that's screaming for your attention? The best way to find that out is to get something pinned down in writing, preferably in one simple, short sentence that says exactly *what you will lose* if this problem isn't solved. Doing this will quickly bring things into the proper perspective for you.

3. *When* must I decide?

Is time a critical factor in your decision? Must you act at once or can you wait without complicating or increasing the possible bad effects of this problem? If you can wait, could be that time alone will solve things for you. Don't, however, use that as an excuse to put things off until tomorrow. Deciding whether to wait or whether to act now is a tough decision in itself and takes a tremendous amount of good judgment on your part.

4. *What else* do I need to know?

Do you have all the facts necessary to make a sound and timely decision? If not, what's missing? Where can you get more information? Who might be able to help you or advise you in reaching your decision? Have you also considered all the consequences or the results of your decision? Will it affect other people? If it will, better check it out with them first.

5. *How* shall I make this decision?

With all these assembled facts—and their consequences—clearly in your mind, set up a balance sheet. Weigh carefully the advantages and the disadvantages of each course of action. A careful comparison of these possible solutions should allow you to pick the right one. Once you've picked it . . . once you've decided on your course of action, then there's only one thing left to do: *Act!*

Why are sound and timely decisions necessary? Because 99 times out of 100 some problem needs solving. If management problems didn't come your way every single day to solve, then you and a lot of other executives would find yourselves out of work and looking for a job. Therefore, since problem-solving is such an important technique for you to learn and since it's really a prerequisite to sound and timely decision making, I'm going to use the rest of this chapter to show you exactly . . .

How To Solve Your Business and Management Problems in Five Easy Steps

1. Assemble all the facts.

The first step in solving your problem so you can make a sound and timely decision is to *gather all the facts bearing on the problem*. How do you go about assembling these facts? Well, according to Carl H. Jordan, an efficiency expert and trouble-shooter for the Winn-Dixie Stores, there are three basic techniques you can use:

"Ask questions. That's the first step," Mr. Jordan says. "If you ask the right people, there's no better way of finding out the facts. You must take the precaution to insure that the person you're asking has no reason *not* to tell you the complete truth. And ask yourself questions, too. You might be pleasantly surprised to find you know some answers yourself.

"Use your eyes and ears. That's the second step. Don't depend entirely on other people. There's no substitute for first-hand observation. What you personally see and hear is often more reliable than second- or third-hand information. There's a precaution to be observed here, too. That is, you should not mix your opinions, your prejudices, or rumors with your facts.

"Read. Reading will greatly expand your knowledge about how to solve problems. Learn how others have solved similar ones. Trade journals are especially useful for they let you concentrate your attention on your own specific field of interest and they devote a great deal of their space to showing how others did it."

2. Test your facts.

After you've assembled all the facts bearing on your problem, your next step is to test each fact by two criteria. You see, some of your so-called facts will be less than accurate. Others will not help you solve your problem. That's why you must now test or recheck every fact.

Your first test should be for accuracy. Are you able to verify second-hand or word-of-mouth information by personal observation? Or by getting the opinion of an expert? Or by experimentation? Do any of your facts contradict each other?

Your second test is for relevance. The quickest way to check a fact for relevance is simply to ask yourself what it contributes to the solution of your problem. If your answer is that it contributes absolutely nothing, if you can solve your problem just as well without it, chances are it's completely irrelevant and useless to you.

3. Getting rid of irrational thoughts.

Doctor William Evans, a New Orleans consulting psychologist, says three mental obstacles tend to get in the way of solving problems.

"These three obstacles are *prejudice, preconceived ideas,* and *emotion,*" Doctor Evans says. "First off, let's look at prejudice.

"*Prejudice makes people look at things improperly.* For instance, my father always thought a man who wore a mustache couldn't be trusted, so whenever he met someone with a mustache, he immediately categorized that person as dishonest!

"Prejudice can keep you from accepting suggestions for improvement from an employee because he's black, not a college graduate, has a redhaired wife, or smokes a pipe. A personnel manager I know has a thing about pipe-smokers. Won't hire anyone for a management job who smokes a pipe. Thinks the person must be too slow, a dreamer, not aggressive enough. Wonder how many good people he's missed hiring because of that prejudice?

"*Then there's the obstacle of preconceived ideas.* Preconceived ideas and prejudice are not the same although preconceived ideas can often lead to prejudice. A preconceived idea or notion keeps a person from accepting the real truth. For instance, cigarette smokers still insist that smoking doesn't cause lung cancer, although there's plenty of evidence to the contrary. Airplanes can't fly—they're too heavy. Space travel is impossible—no Catholic will ever be elected President of the United States—and on and on. To get over this obstacle, ask yourself these questions:

1. Am I just *assuming* something to be true?
2. Do the facts verify my assumption?
3. Is wishful thinking getting in the way?
4. Am I confusing chance with cause and effect?
5. Will my assumption pass the test of logic?

"The last obstacle is emotion," Doctor Evans concludes. "Any feeling—hate, love, fear, suspicion, jealousy—interferes with the evaluation of the facts. A man who's filled with hatred for others sees every day as dark, gloomy, and miserable. A young fellow who's in love sees the sun shining through the clouds even on the rainiest day. The rule here is never study the facts of a problem or try to solve it under emotional stress or strain."

4. Reach a tentative solution.

This is the fourth step in solving your problem. After you've gathered all the facts, after you've weighed them, and after you've viewed them unimpassionedly and scientifically, you should now be able to reach a *tentative solution.*

The best solution should normally be the one with the most advantages and the least disadvantages that will definitely solve your problem for you.

You might come up with 39 different ways to skin a cat; but you want the best one.

5. Put your solution into effect—take the necessary action.

This is the last step in your problem-solving technique. It's usually the biggest obstacle of all because of fear. But to hesitate now is foolish, to say the least. The hard work is over. Don't waver with indecision now. Step right out with confidence and put your corrective action to work at once. After you've decided which solution you're going to use, then put it into effect immediately by issuing the necessary order. Take the appropriate action; put your solution to work for you.

Follow these guidelines—use these techniques—and you'll find you'll be able to make sound and timely decisions. You won't have to call a mass meeting every time you make a decision. You'll learn to acquire all the information possible and then you'll have the courage to say to yourself, "Now it's up to me."

When you do this, a kind of extra muscle will grow on you. You'll get the self-starter's habit of action and leadership. You'll no longer hesitate and beat around the bush. *You'll get things done.*

FIVE

Neglecting to Conduct Personal Inspections Properly

"One of the most neglected areas in management is inspecting the operation," says Walter T. Erwin, Vice-President in Charge of Manufacturing for the Rheem Corporation. "Yet it's one of the most important aspects of your work if you really want to make sure the job gets done.

"A manager can think up a lot of excuses to keep from leaving his desk and going out into the actual working arena. For one thing, he too often construes his primary job to be paper work and his in-box always seems to be overflowing with correspondence that should've been answered yesterday when he gets back from his inspection tour.

"Then he'll always have a stack of telephone messages that piled up during his absence and these have to be taken care of, too. But correspondence and phone calls aren't really the main part of a manager's job at all. They are merely by-products of his real job—red tape that goes along with it. How much a lot of the time depends on him.

"Of course there are several more reasons why, a manager hates to get out from behind his desk to inspect the operation. For instance, many times he simply doesn't have the knowledge he needs to conduct an inspection properly. He doesn't know the actual details of his own operation well enough to really tell when something is wrong and he's afraid of making a fool of himself in front of his own employees. No wonder he doesn't want to leave his office. It's a lot safer there!"

Now what Mr. Erwin says is true, but these problems can

be solved. To become a good inspector, you must know your business inside out. This takes study, planning, and practice. It takes constant study so you will know before you inspect what is correct and what is not correct in your own particular area of responsibility.

It requires planning so you can prepare a schedule of inspections in such a way that over a period of time you'll be able to give your attention to all aspects of your operation. And finally, it takes practice so you'll be able to tell at once what is being done right and what is being done wrong. Yes, it does take a lot of work to conduct a personal inspection properly, but . . .

YOU'LL GAIN THESE BENEFITS WHEN YOU DO

Increased and Improved Production Will Result from Proper Inspections

When you correct improper procedures that you find are costing you time and money, both in employee wages and material costs, you will increase production. An old adage says that *most of the money a businessman calls profit is money he's been able to save in his operation.* Your inspection will help you do that.

Improved Safety Conditions Will Result from Your Inspections

You'll be able to find out which safety rules are sensible and worth while and being obeyed—and which ones are useless and out-of-date and should be got rid of.

Better Housekeeping Is Another Benefit You'll Gain.

I know when you make a tour of your place, people will do a special clean-up job when they know you're coming, but that shouldn't matter to you at all. You should expect them to do that. I'd be disappointed if they didn't. Perhaps it'll be the best way to make sure the place gets a well-needed coat of fresh paint.

You can usually tell by the housekeeping whether the place is under control or not. I suppose it's possible for a plant or department that looks like a pigpen to run like a 21-jewel watch, but it's highly improbable, and to tell the truth, in my personal experience, I've never seen it work that way. If your local foreman or supervisor can't control the things you see on the surface during a brief visit, you know he's let a lot of other more important things slip, too.

You Can Improve Employer-Employee Relationships

Make each inspection a visit, too. Always try to remember first names. Know all you can about the man and what he does. Ask about the health of his wife and children. You might earn five to ten times what he's making, but if you treat him with dignity and respect, you'll get the same in return. Your sincere interest in him will *improve esprit de corps and morale* throughout your organization, and that's a worthwhile dividend, too.

You'll get better over-all results in everything when you know how to conduct a proper inspection, for without a doubt, *an organization does well only that which the boss inspects.*

TECHNIQUES YOU CAN USE TO CONDUCT A PERSONAL INSPECTION

Do the Right People Have the Answers?

Although a plant section manager or a department foreman shouldn't be expected to be a computer and have all the figures in his head, he should at least know roughly what they are, or have them jotted down in his note-book, or know exactly the place where they're to be found.

You can ask such questions as these: "Which department has the highest absenteeism?" "Which section submits the most employee grievances?" "What is the rejection rate of this department's production by quality control?" "Is that above or below other departments?" "Which foreman (supervisor) has the highest production record in the plant?" "Which one has the lowest?" "Which department generates the most scrap?" These questions are general enough to allow a properly informed section manager to answer them easily if he's keeping things under control.

You can set up a rating system something like this to keep track and score your section managers, your foremen, or your supervisors:

6—if the man knows the right answer or has it jotted down in his notebook;

5—if he is able to turn to someone else immediately who does have the answer;

4—if he says, "I don't know, but I'll find out and let you know," and then does just that;

3—if he takes several days (3 or more) to get the information he promised you;

2—if you had to remind him to get the information you asked for;

1—if he still did not give you the information even after you asked for it again, or he gave you the wrong answer;

0—if he says he doesn't know how or where to get the information you want and makes no effort at all to get it.

Although this is not an infallible rating system by any means, you'll soon find that your better managers score from 4 to 6 and your poorest ones score 3 and below. You'll also find that their departments operate at about the same level of efficiency they do. This rating system can also be used as another tool to keep the knowledgeable and capable people moving up in your organization.

Does the Local Manager Really Have Things Under Control?

In every department there are certain functions that can easily be controlled by the manager who's really in charge of things. That's why housekeeping is so often used as a measuring stick to determine the real efficiency of a place. If a department is sloppy and unkempt, you can safely assume the product is handled in exactly the same careless manner.

"Poor housekeeping is primary evidence of lack of control on the part of the store manager," says David Bruce, founder and president of the Consumers Markets, a highly successful midwestern chain of nearly 50 grocery stores. "I've learned to recognize poor housekeeping as the first warning sign of deeper trouble to come. It's a surface symptom of a deep-seated disease.

"And I also know from experience that unless I do something about this problem immediately, my net profit from that store will start to fall. Poor housekeeping, if allowed to continue, will also lead to a higher incident rate in store accidents, both in frequency and severity—for that store's workers will be more careless; they'll knowingly violate safety rules.

"Warehousing procedures will be bad. Canned goods won't be rotated properly. The complete stocking and re-ordering system will break down. They'll have more spoilage of fresh fruits and vegetables. Petty thievery by employees will increase. Business will start to fall off. I've seen it happen too many times.

"I personally look at housekeeping as the basic foundation of good management in a grocery store, and I'm sure it's true in other kinds of businesses, too. I know that if a store manager can't control housekeeping, then it's absolutely impossible for him to *really* have the rest of the place under his complete control."

Check the Obvious Things—They're So Often Overlooked

A gentleman I know conducts a thorough inspection of his car every morning before he leaves his home for work. He starts out by lifting the hood and checking the oil and water level. He inspects the battery. He tugs on the fan belt. Then he starts the motor and lets it warm up while he continues his inspection of windshield wipers, horn, lights and turn signals.

His name is Frank Campbell and he's the president of Campbell Sixty-Six Express, Inc. His trucks with their distinctive picture of a camel stretched out in full gallop and the slogan "Humpin' to Please" on their sides can be seen on all the major highways throughout the midwest.

When Mr. Campbell arrives at work, he spends the first hour or so going over his trucks in the yard the same way he inspected his car at home.

"I check the obvious things because they're so easy to inspect they're often overlooked," Mr. Campbell says. "My service manager knows when a truck is due for its 10 or 20 thousand mile maintenance and he keeps accurate records on all shop work.

"But the thing that can so easily get out of control is the daily first-echelon driver maintenance of the truck. My drivers always keep up with theirs for they know I'll be coming through the yard every single morning without fail. And I use the same system when I inspect my out-of-town branch offices and terminals. I also make a lot of unannounced midnight inspections. That insures the truck being serviced as the driver's last item of work before he goes home for the day."

You can do the same in your own operation, no matter what it is. I know one plant manager who checks the machinery in his plant in much the same way. He leaves the quality of production to his production superintendent, the research and development, and the quality control departments. He finds this to be a very satisfactory way to control his operation.

A Fail-Safe Seven-Step Inspection Procedure

This inspection procedure can be used by anyone in management, from the top to the bottom, but it's especially useful to junior management people such as foremen and front-line supervisors for it gets right down to the nuts and bolts of the operation.

1. Set aside a definite amount of time for daily inspections. Always inspect some phase of your operation every single working day. But don't inspect the same thing at the same time every day. Change things around. Sometimes inspect in the mornings; sometimes in the afternoons. If you have a two- or three-shift operation, do some of your inspecting at night. Don't let anyone home for free!

You'll find that Monday mornings and Friday afternoons are the most critical periods of the week. Or at least the first four hours and the last four hours of your work week are, whatever your schedule is. They're the let-down periods when your employees are more careless and do their worst work. I swear my last two cars were built in one of those two time periods. So bear down on your inspections then more than any other time. The first day of the deer or trout season also falls into that same category.

2. Go over your inspection points before you inspect. Study up and review your selected points of inspection before you inspect. That way you won't get caught short; your employees won't be able to make a fool of you. You'll always appear to be an expert, and in fact, before long you will be. I recommend you select no less than three but no more than eight points to inspect at any one time. By changing these points every day, you'll soon be able to cover your entire operation.

3. Inspect only your selected points. Carefully go over your selected inspection points before you make your inspection. And then when you inspect—*don't look at anything else. Don't try to be the expert on everything in one single day.* You can't do it. Stick to your system and don't let anyone distract you. You'll cover everything in good time.

4. When you inspect—emphasize. Emphasize the points you have selected for your inspection—*not the points your subordinate is trying to emphasize for you.* This can become a cat-and-mouse game if you let it get away from you. Just remember who is inspecting and who is being inspected.

You see, the moment you let your subordinate lead you away from your selected inspection points, you'll no longer be the expert. At that moment you'll be running the risk of exposing your lack of knowledge on the subject your subordinate has selected.

You must retain control of the situation so you can always appear to be the expert. Time, experience, study, and practice will make you one.

5. Always by-pass the chain of authority. This is an absolute must—no exceptions. No other kind of inspection is ever satisfactory. Don't ask your subordinate managers how they're getting along and how things are. You know the answer you'll get. You must go down to the actual working level so you can see for yourself. Of course, as a matter of courtesy the manager of that plant or store, department or section should always go with you, but don't ask him the questions—ask the people who work for him. That's the only way you're going to get straight answers.

6. Ask questions and more questions. Remember that you're inspecting to gain information, not give it out. So ask questions and then listen to the answers. Let your employees tell you how they can improve their own performance. They will if you'll let them. After all, most people want to do the best job they can.

7. Recheck the mistakes you find. An inspection is of no value whatever unless you take the necessary action to correct the mistakes you find. So follow up. Re-inspect. Supervise and make sure your corrective orders are carried out. Remember that an order without supervision is usually the same as no order at all.

How to Be a Tough Inspector and Still Be Liked

I realize that when you are a manager, your job is to manage and supervise people, not win a popularity contest, but it's still a lot better if you can do your job and be liked and respected at the same time. Here are six brief guidelines you can use to attain that goal:

1. Don't take sides with labor against the supervisor or local section manager. This is a cheap way to try to win popularity with all your employees, but it doesn't work out in the long run. Those employees will lose respect, not only for their immediate boss, but also for you. You'll only defeat your purpose in the end.

2. Always praise the supervisor or local section manager. Always support the "boss" in front of his subordinates. Never, never criticize a supervisor or section manager in front of his people. Do that and they'll lose all respect for him. They'll never trust his judgment or have confidence in him again. If he needs to be replaced, then get rid of him. If you're going to keep him in a management slot, then back him to the hilt.

3. Criticize him in private. If things aren't what they should be, take him aside to find fault. Even then, you must criticize with care. Be sure your criticism is both justified and constructive. Don't be vindictive and destructive. And when you do criticize, praise first. It'll take a lot of the sting out when you do.

4. Don't generalize—be specific. If he's guilty, tell him so. Tell him exactly what he's done wrong. Don't take it out on him for something someone else has done. And by the same token, don't try to punish everyone for the mistakes of one individual. Pin the tail on the right donkey.

5. Let the supervisor or local section manager explain his side. Don't criticize until you understand why he's doing it that way. Could be he has a perfectly logical reason for doing things the way he is. Many times local conditions cause the development of certain odd procedures. So find out first before you jump. Give him a chance to explain it to you.

6. Don't harass—inspect. Need I say more?

Here I've given you some guidelines you can use to become adept at making inspections. I'm sure you can come up with some ideas of your own to supplement them. But whatever you do, please keep this one thought clearly in mind:

NEVER INSPECTED—ALWAYS NEGLECTED!

SIX

Failing to Make Sure the Job Is Understood, Supervised, and Accomplished

Sometimes the inability to understand instructions can be traced to improper listening. My wife, for instance, is the world's worst when it comes to receiving instructions on how to get somewhere. Halfway through the instruction she loses patience, waves gaily, and scoots away, invariably turning right where she should've turned left, or completely missing some prominent landmark she's been given for a reference point.

At other times, though, the person giving the directions is guilty of sloppy communication. Not long ago, my son, Larry, ran a classified ad in the Springfield *Leader* to sell his Honda 450 motorcycle. I listened to his directions to the first caller about how to find our house.

"Come down Glenstone to Sunshine," he said. "Go east on Sunshine for two or three miles, south on Ingram Mill for a mile or so, back west on Sunset, south and up the hill on Hillsboro, left on Claremont, right on Avalon, back to the west on Covington which runs into Lomita—it's only a block long, but you can't miss it—yellow brick front—number 31104—goodby."

All this without pausing for a single breath, and then he hung up immediately after he'd finished.

"Did you ask him to repeat your directions?" I asked, knowing that he hadn't.

"No," my son said.

"Do you think he copied down your directions? You were going quite fast, you know."

"I doubt it," Larry said.

"I doubt it, too," I said. "You went too fast for him to do that. If he really wants to buy your motorcycle, he'll have to call back."

Ten minutes later he did. This time my son took it slow and easy and asked questions to make sure his directions were understood before he hung up. (Incidentally, that man did buy the motorcycle.)

Often, managers are just as guilty as my 16-year-old son in assuming their listeners got the message. I'm sure you, too, have at one time or another heard the complaint: "Nobody told me . . . that's not what you said the first time . . . I didn't think you wanted it done this way. . . ."

If you've been having trouble getting your point across, if you've been failing to make sure the job is understood, supervised, and accomplished, this chapter is for you. It'll solve those problems for you. Before I take up the techniques you can use, let me tell you about . . .

SOME OF THE BENEFITS YOU'LL GAIN

People Will Respond Quickly to Your Orders

People will respond at once to orders that are clear, concise, simple, and easy to understand. On the other hand, they can easily become confused if you overstate your order by giving them too many details. Let them do some of the thinking themselves. That way you can emphasize results—not methods, work—not rules. And no matter what your work is, getting people to think for themselves, to use their imagination and initiative, will lead to *a better way of doing things. And that's a benefit, too.*

People Will Do Their Best for You

People will do their best for you when they know exactly what their jobs are and when they know precisely what you want them to do. A great many times a person fails to do a proper job simply because he didn't understand what you wanted done in the first place. Ambiguity, indecisiveness, vagueness, and incompleteness of orders are often to blame for disobedience and failure to comply. It's up to you to tell your people what you expect, when and where you expect it, and then to supervise to make sure the job gets done. Do this and you'll get results; people will do the best they know how for you.

You'll Have More Time for Your Own Work

Not enough time in the day to get things done is a common complaint of businessmen, executives, and managers everywhere. When you make sure the job is understood in the beginning, you won't lose time by repeating that same order over and over again. By the same token, if you make sure the work is properly supervised, you'll cut down on wasteful mistakes and costly repetition. Proper application of those first two steps will lead naturally to the third one: successful completion of the job the first time through. You'll end up with more time for your own work by making sure the other person does his job right the first time.

TECHNIQUES YOU CAN USE TO GAIN THE BENEFITS

Make Sure the Need for an Order Exists

"You don't have to issue an order just to prove you're the boss," says Clifford Dawson, the assistant manager of a J. C. Penney store in Des Moines, Iowa. "If you're in charge of a department or a section, the people who work for you know that already. You don't have to prove it to them by issuing some unnecessary order.

"One of the first things we stress to a new supervisor is for him to make sure he needs an order to actually get something done before he issues it. A great many times, the best test of the efficiency of a department supervisor is not how good he is at bossing other people and issuing orders, but instead, how little he has to tell people what to do because of the way he's organized his work and decentralized his responsibility."

I agree with Cliff a hundred percent. However, I would like to add a few points to his ideas. I know they'll be helpful to you in your job of managing people. The first of these is to—

Issue the Correct Order

A few months ago I was called in as a special consultant to help a plant manager find the reasons behind the low morale of his employees. There were a variety of things to blame, most of them the end result of carelessness and a "don't-give-a-damn-about-labor" attitude on the part of management.

Managers at all levels were issuing unnecessary, improper, and conflicting orders. One I remember specifically because it was such a sore point with all the employees.

The way the plant was physically set up, the cafeteria and the main work area were joined by a long hallway. There was also an outside covered walk between the two that could be used.

Most employees used the outside walk for just a few minutes in the fresh air were a welcome relief, since the temperature in the plant often topped a hundred degrees.

But management stopped the practice of letting their employees use the outside walk (although management still did) and ordered them to use the hot and noisy, crowded and narrow hallway on the way from the plant to the cafeteria and back.

This was an extremely bitter order for the employees to take, and every single one of them mentioned it to me as a clear indication of management's lack of concern for them.

"Why have you issued such an order that keeps your employees from going outside during their break?" I asked the plant manager.

"Because they throw their cigarette butts, cigar stubs, and candy wrappers all over the area," he said. "They act like a bunch of pigs!"

"If that's the only reason you have, then why don't you put butt cans and trash containers along the walk and at the plant and cafeteria entrances?" I asked. "Then instead of issuing an order your people despise you for, you can issue an order to *please use the butt cans and trash containers*. They'll obey that order for it means they'll be able to use the outside walk when they do."

He followed my suggestion and the icy barriers between management and labor began to melt away. You see, a sensible correct order will usually be obeyed without question, but all of us rebel at an order we feel is unfair and unjust.

Never Issue an Order You Can't Enforce

One of the best ways to retain the upper hand as a manager is never to issue an order you can't enforce. I know of nothing more disastrous than to have an employee refuse to obey an order that you're not capable of backing up or enforcing.

You should also remember that sometimes a person won't carry out your order because he doesn't know how. Arthur Ingram, now the president of Ingram Industries, a computer manufacturing firm in Dallas, Texas, tells about this personal incident that happened to him.

"It's absolutely essential that you never give orders that are beyond the capacity of the person to carry out," Arthur says. "I remember an especially embarrassing experience from my early days as a department supervisor. A young fellow had been hired as an inspector for my department. We were rushed and way behind schedule, so when he reported for duty, I handed him a micrometer and put him to work at once.

" 'Mac, check the thickness of those discs,' I told him. 'If they measure more than four thousandths, throw 'em out. And hurry, the whole darned assembly line is held up waiting for them. I'll be back in a little while to see how you're doing.'

"Half an hour later I came back to check on his progress. Not a single disc had been checked. Mac was standing there, embarrassed to death, red-faced, staring at the micrometer.

" 'What the hell's wrong!' I yelled. 'Why haven't you done anything?'

" 'Because I don't know how to use this kind of micrometer,' he said. 'I've never seen one like it before.' "

To keep yourself from getting into a bind like that, I'd suggest you use the method I do. I always ask the person first if he knows how to do a certain job. If he says he does, then I ask him if he'll be good enough to go ahead and do it. If he says he doesn't know how, then I ask him what he can do. When he tells me, I ask him if he'll do that. That way, I can't miss.

Disguise Your Orders As Suggestions or Requests

Along that same line, I'll say that if your people have any initiative whatever, they'll respond much faster and you'll get far better results from suggestions than from dictatorial orders. Used to be the only place people reacted without question to direct commands was in the army, but in the past few years even that's changed.

If you've been used to barking out orders of "Do this!" "Do that!", you'll find it's an extremely pleasant change of pace to say, "Would you be good enough to . . . ," "I wish you would . . . ," "Please. . . ." In fact, you'll find such new methods can do wonders for your peptic ulcer.

Know What You Want Before You Issue an Order

It's important to know what you want before you tell any-one to do anything. Too many orders grow like a rambling rose, creeping ivy, or the crab grass in my yard. If you aren't sure of the results you want, then you're not yet ready to issue an order.

To help you determine the results you want first, follow these simple guidelines each time so you can establish the right thinking pattern:

1. *What* exactly is it I want to get done?
2. *Who* is going to do this job?
3. *When* does the job have to be done?
4. *Why* does it have to be done?
5. *Where* is the best place to do it?
6. *How* will it be done?

If you box yourself into a corner by forcing yourself to answer such relevant questions of *what, who, when, why, where, how,* there's no doubt about it. You can't help but improve your abilities to make sure the job is understood, supervised, and accomplished.

Use Clear, Concise, Simple Language

I've always had a thing about people who use big words just to confuse or impress other people. I admit it's a special gripe of mine. I personally feel *you should not only say a thing in such a way that you can be understood, but you should also say it in such a way that it is impossible to be misunderstood.* Here are four ways to do just that:

Be brief.   Say only as much as you need to say—no more. Save your idle chatter for coffee breaks. If you can explain your point in two sentences—use two. Don't worry about the left-over white space on the page. If it bothers you that much, cut it off.

Use short words and short sentences.   Short words and short sentences promote understanding. Don't worry, your letter won't sound like a first grade reader. I use simple words and short sentences all the time and no one's ever accused me of writing books for elementary school students. There are lots of small words that can say all the things you want to say—and then some.

Use one sentence for each idea.   Don't drag your sentences on and on without end. Start a new sentence for each new idea. That's the rule—just like that. It's that simple.

Be specific.   Don't use *they* said or *they* want. That's another one of my pet peeves. *Who* said? *Who* wants it? Name names. Give figures. Quote facts. Give examples.

Have Oral Orders Repeated Back to You

"Following this simple rule does two things for you," says Stanley Adams, a hardware store owner in Tacoma, Washington. "First of all, you know for sure whether your listener got your instructions correct or not. Second, it gives you a chance to check on yourself so you'll know if you actually said what you wanted to say."

To tell the truth, I can think of no exception to this rule whatever. First time you break it, so help me, things'll go wrong. Never fails. And if people do misunderstand, it's impossible for you to make sure the job is understood, supervised, and accomplished, now isn't it?

Use Your Established Chain of Authority to Issue Orders

No matter how big or how small the organization, it always has a definite fixed chain or line of authority through which orders, commands, or instructions are transmitted.

If you have any question in your mind about who works for whom in your company or who you do or don't take orders from or give orders to, then study your organization chart. It'll clarify things for you.

It's absolutely essential that you use this line of authority when you issue instructions. To bypass the foreman or the supervisor or the section chief is not only a violation of good management procedure, but it can also be confusing to the employee if the orders you issue happen to conflict with those he's received previously from his immediate superior. *No man can serve two masters,* and that's as true today as it was two thousand years ago when Christ first said it.

Encourage Questions from Your Subordinates

Whenever you issue an order, be it oral or written, you should encourage questions. I know some people hesitate to ask for clarification of doubtful points because of the possibility of exposing their ignorance.

I've never worried much about that. A college history professor, Doctor Warren Flanders, helped me get over that fear a long time ago.

"If you've got a question, don't hesitate to ask it," Doctor Flanders would say. "If I haven't made the point clear to just one of you, chances are there are others who don't understand it either. So ask your questions. If people laugh, don't worry; they're not laughing at you. They're probably laughing at my inability to give proper instruction."

Ask Them Questions, Too.

If your subordinates don't ask questions, you can ask them questions yourself. Let me preface this point by saying that whenever you issue oral orders that have more than three main points to remember, you should always have your listeners take notes.

Then you can ask questions like this without hurting anyone's feelings: "Jack, would you look at your notes there—did I say two or three?" You know what you said; you just want to make sure that Jack and everybody else knows.

Supervise—Supervise—Supervise . . .

Always remember that an order without supervision is no order at all. You don't have to personally supervise every detail of the work when you're a manager. That's impossible.

Use your foremen, your department supervisors, your section chiefs to inspect and supervise. You should supervise them; they should supervise the actual operation and the minute details. Have them report the progress of the work to you.

If you want to personally supervise some aspect of the job —and you should do that, you know—then follow the guidelines I gave you in the last chapter on how to conduct a personal inspection of the work. There's no better way to supervise than to inspect when you really know what you're looking for.

Making sure the job is understood, supervised, and accomplished is one of the biggest barriers you'll encounter as a manager. Use the techniques I've given you here as a basic foundation to work from and you'll be able to conquer this obstacle easily.

SEVEN

Wasting Time on Details or Work That Belongs to Others

A certain gentleman I know has been president of a mid-western bank for more than 30 years now. He *personally* approved the first loan I ever made there back in the thirties—a two hundred dollar college loan—and he also *personally* approved the last loan I made there when I bought a vacation cottage on Lake of the Ozarks last summer. (And that, no doubt, will be the last loan he ever makes to me if he happens to read this chapter!)

The bank has doubled in size and doubled again during those years, yet he has followed the same routine every morning of *personally* sorting and opening every single piece of mail and distributing it to his officers, tellers, and other bank employees.

Does this sound unusual or far-fetched to you? Well, it isn't. Another bank president I know requires his Board of Directors to approve all loans of $100 and above at their regular weekly meetings. The Board often has little sound basis for arriving at a logical decision; it usually has to depend on the recommendation of one of the bank officers who knows the loan applicant. I'm sure you'll agree that their time and the president's time is wasted on details and work that could more profitably be given to someone else to do.

Or take that first bank president again. He might at least have given some clerk the authority to open and distribute the bank's mail. He might also have appointed one of his vice-presidents to be in charge of all small loans below a certain reasonable figure.

Had he done that, he'd have had more time to analyze his bank's new business opportunities, to study his biggest customer's operations, to use his more than 30 years of valuable banking experience to help his vice-presidents solve their problems, and to make friends with the owners and top management of new businesses—and therefore, potential new customers—who'd moved to town.

BENEFITS YOU CAN GAIN BY NOT WASTING TIME ON DETAILS OR WORK THAT BELONGS TO SOMEONE ELSE

You'll Gain Respect from Your Employees

When you trust people enough to let them carry out the details of their own work, they'll respect you and have confidence in you. Whenever you show you have faith in a person's ability to do the job, you'll find he needs far less supervision. He'll be motivated to do the best job he can for you. In fact, he'll work whether you're around to watch him or not; he'll not let you down.

You'll Develop Initiative and Resourcefulness in People

When you give a person the opportunity to do his own work without interference from you, he'll be anxious to show you that your trust is well placed. He'll use his imagination and initiative to get the job done. He'll develop his ingenuity and resourcefulness. His honest and sincere efforts to do a decent job for you will contribute greatly to your own individual success as a manager.

You Won't Have a Bunch of Yes-Men Around You

When you don't try to dominate others, when you don't waste your time on the details of someone else's work, you'll get rid of the yes-men in your organization. And that's a distinct and definite advantage to you. You see, a domineering and over-forceful boss drives away subordinates with imagination and initiative.

If you insist on doing everything yourself, your best people will leave you, but your worst ones will stay and let you do the work for them. If you want to gain the benefit of not having any yes-men in your organization, then think of your people as working *with* you—not *for* you—and treat them the same way.

TECHNIQUES YOU CAN USE TO GAIN THE BENEFITS

Concentrate on Your Own Primary Management Responsibilities

It's difficult to concentrate on your own primary management responsibilities if they haven't been defined for you. Now admittedly, I couldn't begin to tell you what your specific duties are, say as a production superintendent in the ABC Rubber Company, but I can tell you about your management responsibilities in such a way that you'll be better able to carry out your own individual managerial duties when you finish this particular section.

To begin with, let me say that management is the process whereby the resources of people, money, material, time, and facilities are all used to accomplish the primary mission of an organization, no matter what it is. Is that what management means to you? That's what it should mean, at any rate.

Now the specific functions of management include planning, organizing, coordinating, and controlling those resources in such a way as to accomplish the mission in the most profitable way possible. Do any of these functions sound familiar to you? They should.

Finally, the actual detailed duties of an executive or manager should include establishing job objectives, motivating people to reach those goals, making and communicating decisions, introducing new concepts and new ideas, maintaining cooperation, and developing your subordinates to assume more and higher responsibilities.

If all this sounds new or strange to you, if these specific detailed duties of a manager I've just given you don't sound like your own job description, then please keep right on reading. Chances are you're wasting good managerial time and talent on details or work that definitely belongs to someone else.

A Manager Must Decentralize Execution of the Work

"A manager must decentralize execution of the actual work to be done, or he isn't doing his job properly," says

Paul DeWitt, Office Manager for the Armco Metal Building Company of Memphis, Tennessee. "Since the manager has foremen and supervisors, department heads and section chiefs, secretaries and clerks working for him, it follows that he cannot do everything himself, nor is he expected to. If he could, a lot of other people would be out of a job.

"A manager has his own heavy responsibilities. He must plan, make decisions, communicate them, order, and supervise. To fulfill his own responsibilities, he must assign specific tasks to others to do. He should also give his people a reasonable latitude to choose their own methods of doing the job. Each of his subordinates should feel completely free to act within the limits of his delegated responsibility and authority."

Not all managers are capable of doing this good a job of decentralizing the work of others. Some are prone to do far too much by themselves and leave too little responsibility and initiative for their subordinates. But that is the road to small achievement. Your ultimate success as a manager will depend upon each individual under you having a specific job to do and a definite responsibility to fulfill that will tax him to the utmost —and upon your seeing that he does them both.

Then there is the manager who is prone to do too little— the one who decides, plans, and orders—but then sits back as if his job were all done and waits for his subordinates to complete the assignment he has given them.

But to neglect supervision is also another road that leads to small achievement. To succeed as a manager, you must oversee the operation of your plans and the work of your subordinates—coordinating, adjusting, and controlling as necessary— but at the same time, permitting them to do their own work without interference from you.

How to Give Freedom and Still Keep Control

"Fear causes a lot of managers to hang on to the details of work that belong to their subordinates," says Gene Garrison, foreman in charge of production of the Household Soap and Detergent Division of the Colgate-Palmolive Company in Jersey City, New Jersey.

"They're afraid that if they delegate responsibility and authority to their people, something will happen that could seriously endanger their position. They imagine all sorts of problems and troubles that could come up if they surrender any part of their responsibilities to their subordinates."

The kind of manager Gene describes is quite common. To tell the truth, most of us feel we could do a better job of it than anyone else. And a lot of us look at delegation of authority and responsibility as a loss of control. But it doesn't have to work that way at all.

You see, the smart manager will delegate responsibility for the work and the necessary authority to carry it out *only after he has established the proper control measures that will allow him to take immediate corrective action if things do go* wrong. Here's what those control measures are:

1. Your employee must first be thoroughly trained, qualified, and capable of doing the job.
2. He should be given his responsibilities, not all at once, but in increments, step by step.
3. You should correct his mistakes and praise his successes as he proceeds with his new assignments and responsibilities.
4. At each critical point, you should have your controls set up in such a way that you can move in at once to stop or take over any action that might seriously jeopardize successful completion of the job or that might endanger either yours or your employee's position.

Remember that to delegate the responsibility and the authority for the details of the job will build a feeling of self-confidence in your subordinate. It's definite proof that you have faith in him and in his abilities.

Do this, and you give him the chance for individual expression. You've given him a chance to learn and the opportunity to make a contribution that he can call his own. You've helped him grow; he'll be a better employee for you.

Delegation of Responsibility Is a Sign of Good Management

"To delegate responsibility for the details of the work to your subordinates is a sign of good management," says Price Jennings, Shipping Department Supervisor for the Amway Corporation, in Ada, Michigan. "You are not a manager if you do not delegate responsibility, just as you are not a pianist if you do not play the piano, or a machinist if you cannot operate a machine.

"If you insist on keeping your hand in the details all the time, you'll discourage your subordinates by competing with them. And then, the capable ones will leave you; the weak ones will sit back and let you do all the work. In the end you'll have no time left for your real job as a manager—thinking, planning, organizing, controlling."

To sum up this idea, let me say that the manager who fails to delegate endangers his position far more than the one who doesn't. If you try to do it all yourself, you'll have to—for you'll have no one but yourself to do it. Or as the president of one company so succinctly told his personnel manager: "Find the guy we can't get along without and then fire him! I'm scared to death of him if he's indispensable, what would we do if he died?"

Use Mission-Type Orders

One of the best ways I know to keep yourself from meddling in details or doing the work that belongs to others, and to develop initiative in your subordinates at the same time, is to use mission-type orders.

What is a mission-type order? Well, quite simply said, *a mission-type order tells a person what you want done, but it doesn't tell him how to do it.* The *how-to* is left entirely up to him.

A mission-type order says what your desired results are, but it doesn't tell your subordinate the methods he must use to gain them for you. It emphasizes skill—not rules.

When you use this kind of an order, you open the door wide for your employee to use his initiative, his imagination, and his ingenuity to solve the problem you've given him.

If you've never used mission-type orders before, you're going to be pleasantly surprised when you do, for they'll give your organization a flexibility you never thought possible before.

This will be especially apparent if you've been used to running a one-man show and not letting your subordinates carry out the details of the work. You'll suddenly find you have better people working for you than you thought you had.

The Format for a Mission-Type Order

A mission-type order is composed of three basic elements: (1) the mission to be accomplished or the problem to be solved, (2) the limitations imposed, (3) the resources available.

1. *The mission to be accomplished or the problem to be solved* must be clearly and concisely stated in your order. You should say precisely what it is that you want done.

2. *The limitations imposed* must also be pointed out in your order. In other words, how far can your subordinate go in his methods to carry out your order, to accomplish the mission, or to solve the problem you've given him. What limitations, if any, have you placed on him, or does he have free rein all the way?

If this is a new idea to you, a good rule of thumb you can use is to *balance the welfare of your people against the accomplishment of the mission.* When you do this, you'll eliminate most of the questions you have in your mind as to the limitations you should place on your subordinate.

3. *The resources available* must also be spelled out precisely in your order. Your subordinate must know exactly what he can use to accomplish the mission for you. If you'll remember, when we talked about concentrating on your own primary management responsibilities, we said that the resources available to a manager to get the job done were *people, money, material, time,* and *facilities.*

Here, then, you must spell out in exact and definite terms the actual resources you're going to make available to your subordinate to get the job done. If, for example, you're going to ask a man to get a job done in two days that would normally take three, you'll have to give him the authority for over-time. This would immediately require the use of *people, money, time, facilities*—four of the five resources management uses to get the job done.

What a Mission-Type Order Will Not Do for You

A mission-type order is not a cure-all. It will not do everything for you. The one thing it will not do for you is this: *it will not tell your subordinate how to do the job.* The *how* of it must be left up to him, for the moment you tell him how to do the job, you no longer have a mission-type order at all.

Tell a man how to do the details of his work, and you've taken away his flexibility completely. He can't use his ingenuity, his initiative, or his good judgment to solve your problem for you.

To tell the truth, if you can't use mission-type orders, I don't see how you can be a successful manager. In fact, you wouldn't need people to do the work for you at all; you'd need only robots or machines.

In the Final Analysis . . .

"Mission-type orders will separate the men from the boys, and that's for sure," says Henry Schroeder, Assistant Manager of the Research and Development Division of Midwest Electric Corporation in St. Paul, Minnesota. "Mission-type orders will weed out the ribbon clerks for you. That's especially true in a department like ours where people are paid to be creative thinkers. Your best people will learn to use their heads, to make their own decisions, to figure out their own courses of action.

"When you use mission-type orders, you'll quickly get rid of the inefficient and incompetent subordinates in your company before they can become a burden to you. If you do have junior executives and young managers in your organization who can't handle mission-type orders, get rid of them, and do it quickly. Replace them with people who can."

The simple truth of the matter is this: the subordinate who isn't motivated to do a better job for you working under mission-type orders isn't worth his pay to you at all. You're better off without him.

I'd like to sum up what I've said in this chapter like this: About two thousand years ago, Horace, a famous Roman poet, said, "I mind the business of other people, having lost my own." If you follow the guidelines I've given you in this chapter, you won't find yourself in that dilemma.

EIGHT

Refusing to Assess Your Own Performance Realistically

I've always found myself incapable of appraising my own performance of duty honestly and realistically if I had to use one of those report forms with blocks or squares to put checkmarks or *X*'s in.

It's hard enough for me to use such a form in grading the efficiency of a subordinate, especially when I'm asked to determine the fine points of difference between *exemplary* and *outstanding* or *excellent* and *superior*.

But it's absolutely impossible for me to use such a form to assess the quality of my own work and be completely honest with myself when I do. I simply cannot base my subjective opinions on objective facts if I have to give an adjectival rating of my own performance of duty. To tell the truth, I suppose I'm just too biased in favor of myself.

I have, however, developed a set of simple questions that I've found to be much more practical in assessing my own performance honestly. Almost all of them can be answered with one word—*Yes* or *No*. And I can tell quickly enough if I'm really doing the job I'm being paid to do or not by the way I answer them. Here's what those questions are:

1. Do you give your boss problems or solutions?
2. Do you try to get all the facts first?
3. Do you use all available resources to get the job done?
4. Do you try to slough off the details?
5. Do you panic easily?
6. Are your reports based on actual results?

7. Do you meet deadlines?
8. Do you finish the job?

Now before we discuss these questions in detail, I'd like first to mention a few of the . . .

BENEFITS YOU'LL GAIN WHEN YOU DO ASSESS YOUR OWN PERFORMANCE OF DUTY HONESTLY AND REALISTICALLY

You'll Learn to Be Honest with Yourself

It's highly important when you're assessing your own performance of duty that you tell yourself the truth. If you do want to improve, you must be honest with yourself. To lie to yourself at a time like this will accomplish nothing for you at all.

Shakespeare said it better, perhaps, than anyone else when he said, "This above all: to thine own self be true, and it must follow, as the night the day, thou canst not then be false to any man." I don't see how I can improve on that at all, and I'm certainly not going to try.

You'll Consolidate Your Strengths and Eliminate Your Weakness

You should evaluate yourself so you'll know your own strengths and weaknesses. You can never become a truly successful manager until you know your own capabilities and limitations and are, in fact, the master of yourself.

When you make an honest inventory of both your good and bad points, when you recognize your strengths and realize your weaknesses, you've taken an important step toward assessing yourself and your own performance on the job realistically. You'll be far better prepared for promotion than your contemporaries when you do this.

You Can Rid Yourself of a Manager's Greatest Fear

The fear of failure hangs over most managers; this fact has been revealed by hundreds of psychological evaluations. But many managers will not readily admit their fear of failure, for in their minds doing so would be a sign of weakness.

Wiser managers, however, are able to appraise their anxieties honestly and to master them effectively. The fundamental starting point from which you can conquer this basic fear of failure is an honest self-inventory and the assessment of your own performance realistically.

TO ASSESS YOUR OWN PERFORMANCE REALISTICALLY ASK YOURSELF THESE QUESTIONS

Do You Give Your Boss Problems or Solutions?

You have problems enough of your own to solve without having your subordinates bring you their problems to take care of, too. Your boss feels the same way. This is not to say that you shouldn't turn to your superior for help when you need it, but you should not bring him only your problem. Bring him a couple of tentative solutions he can choose from.

"I keep my eye on a subordinate who brings me a proposed solution or two with his problem," says Alfred Stone, Executive Vice-President of Burlington Industries, a business machines manufacturing company in Chicago, Illinois. "Chances are he's a comer, a doer, as well as a thinker.

"A lot of people come to me in the middle of a project to tell me about some difficult problem they've run into. Unfortunately, they offer no solution, not even a poor one. Just thinking about the problem seems to have taken all their time. And whether they realize it or not, they're asking me to use my time to solve their problems. They want me to do their thinking for them, and I simply don't have the time to do that.

"The subordinate I earmark for promotion may also bring difficult problems to my attention, but he always brings at least one solution, usually two, along with it. Normally, one of them will do the trick."

So next time you take a question to your boss, take along some possible answers, too. Best way in the world to let him know that you're a comer, a doer, and a thinker.

Do You Try to Get All the Facts First?

"Sometimes it's a mistake to always be first with an answer unless you know for sure it's the right answer. Speed doesn't always indicate accuracy," says John Newman, Chief of the

Laboratory Section of the Cox Medical Center in San Diego, California. "In fact, it can often mean the opposite, especially in lab work.

"Young technicians new on the job are always anxious to be first, thinking it will please the boss. Of course, we can't waste any time here; we're always overloaded with work. But I always impress my people with the idea that unless their reports are accurate, they're actually worse than useless. A patient's life can depend on us."

Without a doubt, the least glamorous part of any job is the minutiae—the seemingly never-ending, and many times deadly monotonous, details. But before you start giving answers to your boss, you must acquaint yourself with enough details to make sure your answer is right. I'll have even more to say about the details of your work a little later.

At any rate, don't neglect your homework; base your recommendations on the facts. There's an old adage that fits quite well here, I think, which says, "The hurrier I go, the behinder I get."

Do You Use All Available Resources to Get the Job Done?

Another good way to impress your boss is to use every means at your disposal to get the job done. Never go back to him for help as long as you can get it somewhere else.

If you've been going to your boss every time you reach an impasse, only to hear answers like these, "You can find the answer to your question in the file on that subject . . . ," "I sent out a memo to all departments explaining that point just last week . . . ," "Go over your notes from yesterday's meeting; I discussed it in complete detail then," chances are you're not using all your resources at hand to get the job done.

However, if you rarely go to him with questions when you're working on an assignment he's given you—if you get as many answers as you can before the job starts—if you've made sure you know his thinking and his point of view on the matter, you're doing the right thing. And you can be sure of this: your boss will know it, too.

Do You Try to Slough Off the Details?

There's a big difference between delegating responsibility for the detailed work that belongs to someone else and sloughing off the details that you ought to be doing yourself. If you'll remember, I gave you some concrete guidelines in the last chapter that you could use to keep from wasting time on details or work that belongs to others. But I don't want you to use those guidelines as an excuse to get rid of the details of the work that you yourself are actually responsible for.

If you really want to get the job done—if you really are a doer, not just a noise-maker—you won't run away from the details that really belong to you. But if you're the kind who wants to deal only with the big picture and let others handle all your time-consuming and nerve-wracking details, chances are you're guilty of violating this one.

For instance, I've had would-be writers come up to me after one of my lectures and say, "Tell me now, you don't really have to worry too much about your punctuation, your grammar, and that sort of thing when you write, do you? You know, I mean, if you really have something worth while to say, the editor will take care of those minor details, won't he?"

My answer is always quite blunt. *"No, he won't."* If you're careless about your punctuation, your grammar, your spelling, and your word usage, your editor can legitimately suspect that you're careless about your facts, too. Besides, that's not his job; it's yours.

I was 45 years old when I wrote my first book, *How to Use the Dynamics of Motivation.** Before I wrote it, I spent nearly a year reviewing all those tiresome details of grammar and punctuation I'd learned away back in high school but had forgotten during all those intervening years.

Sure I miss sometimes. I'm not letter perfect, but after all, who is? However, I'm truly gratified and I do feel I've done my part when I get a letter like this from one of my readers:

> "You know I enjoyed your book, *How to Put Yourself Across with People,*** or I wouldn't be writing to

---

* James K. Van Fleet, *How to Use the Dynamics of Motivation* (West Nyack, New York: Parker Publishing Company, 1967).

** James K. Van Fleet, *How to Put Yourself Across with People* (West Nyack, New York: Parker Publishing Company, 1971).

you . . . I thank you for writing in a language so under-
standable. . . . Yours is the first book I've found easy
to digest on the first reading. . . ."

I'd never have received a letter like that had I not made
the honest effort to learn all those tedious and time-consuming
details of how to write simply, concretely, and to the point.

Do You Panic Easily?

It's easy enough to work and get a job done when things
are going smoothly and there are no problems. Anyone can do
that. But the rough days with obstacles and problems provide
the real testing ground.

"To remain calm under fire and not lose your head is one
of the most important qualifications a manager must have,"
says George V. Osborne, Vice-President in Charge of the Overseas Marketing Division of the Cal-Tex Oil Company.

"Not long ago we were looking for a man to take on an
important overseas assignment in the Orient. A lot of our
young junior executives were being considered. All of them had
the necessary educational qualifications and technical knowledge. I had the responsibility of making the final selection.

"As I say, all of them were pretty evenly matched. But in
the end I chose the man who could take the most unexpected
things completely in stride without losing his head or getting
rattled."

If you can remain calm and keep your cool under conditions that would cause the average man to lose his poise, his
nerve, or his temper, you'll certainly be worthy of the opportunity for additional responsibility, too. If you can do that,
you'll be getting things done while others around you are running for cover.

Are Your Reports Based on Actual Results?

Production reports, sales reports, construction reports, and
the like should tell what you've actually done, the results you've
obtained. Your boss isn't at all interested in how much trouble
you've had in getting the job done unless you've wasted company resources. He's interested only in results, and that's all
your report should tell him.

So quiz yourself thoroughly on this point. A written report can often tell a great deal about you to your boss. Your company may have certain specific requirements, certain ground rules you must follow, but I know I'm safe in saying that, in general, you'll be smart to skip all the background, the plans you've made, the tactics you used, the problems you encountered, the headaches you had. Don't turn a progress report into a television soap-opera trying to gain sympathy. Just tell what you've done in as few words as possible.

Reports are essential, of course. They're a necessary part of business and management. But please remember this point if you will: A long, involved, and detailed report is often nothing more than a substitute for action; the person who gets the job done often says little but does much.

Do You Meet Deadlines?

Rare is the manager who can get the job done or accomplish his goals without watching the clock and the calendar. *When* something is done is often just as important as *what* is done.

"You can't dry today's wash in yesterday's sun," is as applicable to a manager as to a housewife. A solution that was perfect for yesterday's problem might be completely worthless today.

"I can't use a man who doesn't get his work done on time," says Sidney Thompson, Controller and chief finance officer of the Collins Radio Corporation in Cedar Rapids, Iowa. "No matter how complete and accurate his work might be, if I can't depend on him to get it done on time, I just can't use that person in my department. Budget and fiscal work demands people who can meet deadlines and work under pressure."

If you're going to meet deadlines yourself, you should never take your eye off the target date. If unforeseen obstacles or problems come up, report that fact to your superior so you can review the due date and perhaps change it. But don't use that as an excuse to drag your feet and put things off. And above all, don't leave your boss stranded on deadline day by not getting your report in to him on time.

Do You Finish the Job?

Starting a job is a lot easier than finishing it. The early phases of thinking about a new project, getting your ideas down on paper, talking to your associates and colleagues about it are exciting. But as that first flush of excitement fades away, tedious details and problems start to creep in.

So it's up to you to check on your own staying power. One way you can do this is to keep a running inventory of your current jobs that aren't finished. Keep track of when they were given to you, when you started to work on them, what the projected completion dates are, and see if you're keeping up or not.

If you're tending to drift along and let things slide by, could be you fit the category of manager that Earl Kirkpatrick, President of the First National Bank of Atlanta, Georgia, had in mind, when he described one of his assistants who starts but never seems to finish any job.

"Sam starts out like a house on fire," Earl says. "But that's about as far as he ever seems to get. A couple of weeks later he's added that new project to a couple of dozen other jobs he'll probably never complete."

In fact, to insure that you do finish each job you start, you'll need persistence, a persistence that President Calvin Coolidge once described this way: "Nothing in the world can take the place of persistence," he said. "Talent will not; nothing is more common than unsuccessful men with talent. Genius will not; the world is full of educated derelicts. Persistence and determination alone are omnipotent. The slogan 'Press on!' has solved and always will solve the problems of the human race."

If you have that kind of persistence, no doubt about it—you'll finish every single job you start.

How to Analyze Your Own Performance of Duty

The quickest way for you to analyze your own performance of duty is to answer these same questions honestly:

1. Do you give your boss problems or solutions?
2. Do you try to get all the facts first?

3. Do you use all available resources to get the job done?
4. Do you try to slough off the details?
5. Do you panic easily?
6. Are your reports based on actual results?
7. Do you meet deadlines?
8. Do you finish the job?

If you answered the first question with the word "solutions," the second, third, sixth, seventh, and eighth with "yes," the fourth and fifth with "no," then you're a doer, not a noisemaker—and that's good, for about the finest reputation you can build is to have it said of you that *you get things done.* You'll become known as a *can-do* person who can be depended on to actually get the job done—no matter what.

Business and industry are always looking for people who can get the job done. Such individuals are always sought after for they are so few in number that they're always highly appreciated.

Use the eight questions I've given you in this chapter to analyze and assess your own performance of duty honestly and realistically, and you can be one of those can-do people, too.

NINE

Accepting the Minimum Instead of Going for the Maximum

Not long ago George Orr, manager of the Dayton Rubber and Tire Company's Springday plant, was telling me about a foreman he'd let go because he couldn't be motivated to give his best to the job.

"Hank had a *civil service* outlook about his work," George said. "He thought promotion should be based on seniority instead of performance. In fact, when a couple of younger foremen were promoted and Hank wasn't, he complained bitterly about our promotion policies. Said he *outranked* both men and that we weren't giving his seniority with the company proper consideration!

"Hank was also a privilege counter. Oh, he wouldn't ask for privileges he wasn't entitled to, but he always made sure to ask for everything he thought he had coming to him.

"And was he ever a clock-watcher. Why, you could set your watch by him. He was always right on time in the morning —never one minute early and never one minute late, but right on the dot. And he always made sure to leave right on the stroke of five in the afternoon, too. Hank always put in exactly 40 hours a week—not a moment less, but never a moment more either.

"He was good on paperwork, I will say that. He made sure his production reports, quality control reports, salvage reports, attendance records, and so on were accurate, neat, and turned in on time. Hank believed in following the book right to the letter no matter what the outcome. If that didn't produce the desired results, then he felt he couldn't be blamed for he'd followed the rules.

"But as a department manager, he never really made anything happen. He never made his influence felt. Nor did he ever come up with any ideas or suggestions on how to improve· or increase his department's production.

"Oh, he always made his weekly quota of 30 right on the nose, but that was it. He met exactly his quota—but not one bit more. And frankly speaking, I think his department would've done that whether he was there or not.

"And everything else in Hank's department just barely met rock-bottom minimum standards, too. For instance, he had the most machine down-time for it took him longer than anyone else to get a broken-down machine back into operation again. And instead of putting the crew to work on something more productive, Hank's standard solution was always to have them sweep and scrub the floor or wash the windows.

"His spoilage rate was higher—his department had more minor accidents—he led the plant in the number of union grievances—his output per hourly wage dollar was 14 percent lower than anyone else.

"But we can't operate Springday at minimum levels of efficiency. Our goal is to become the biggest rubber plant in the business. To attain that goal, everyone has to give everything he's got. He has to give his maximum. We must have managers and executives, foremen and supervisors who are enthusiastic and positive: men who want to push our company clear to the top.

"So when a better man came along, I let Hank go. With his attitude, I figured he'd be much better off if he could get a civil service job working for the government, and in fact, I told him so. I guess he took my advice for I understand he's with the post office now as a mail carrier. That's a good job for him; he'll get a raise there every couple of years even though he keeps doing the same work. All he has to do is deliver the mail and keep his nose clean."

Well, as George says, some people can't be motivated to do more than the minimum no matter what. But I also know that most of the time managers accept just average or even minimum performance simply because they don't know how to inspire and motivate people to give their utmost.

After my conversation with George that day I went home and put my memory machine to work. I came up with quite a few techniques that I've used successfully over the years to get the best out of people.

You can use these same techniques to get the maximum response from your people, too. I'm not going to say you can use them all on every person, nor am I going to say they'll all work on every person. You must be selective in your approach. Tailor your methods to fit the person. When you do . . .

YOU'LL GAIN THESE BENEFITS

1. You won't have to accept the minimum from people.
2. People will give their maximum efforts for you.
3. Production and/or sales will go up.
4. Costs and expenses will go down.
5. This means increased profit, prestige, promotion, or all three for you.

TECHNIQUES YOU CAN USE TO GAIN THESE BENEFITS

Set a High Standard of Performance for Your Organization

What you do, what you say, and how you yourself act will have a major bearing on whether you're able to get the maximum efforts from your employees or not. If you give only the minimum yourself to the job, you have no right to expect the maximum effort from them.

Just for instance, if you straggle in to work late and leave early; if you're careless about the quality of your men's work— not interested in the amount of production or its quality—not concerned about waste; if you act bored to death with your own job; then your people will no doubt assume the identical attitude about their work, too.

But if you set the right example by giving the maximum yourself, your employees will do the same. Enthusiasm is contagious. If you're positive, enthusiastic, and excited about your work, chances are your employees will feel that way, too.

"I've never met a successful manager of people who was not highly motivated himself," says William A. Doane, Safety Director for the Phillips Petroleum Company. "The best motivators of men are those people who are themselves hard workers almost to the point of maximum commitment to their work.

"Managers like these motivate their people largely by example. And employees like to feel they're living up to the high standards the boss sets himself, especially when he's giving his maximum effort to the job of making his department successful."

Don't Accept the Present System As the Best or Only Way

A lot of people are the victims of *status-quo thinking*. Just because they've always done a certain job a certain way, they assume it's the best possible method, perhaps the only one. So they resist change. They find the idea they must alter their behavior or their thought patterns in some way not only uncomfortable, but sometimes even frightening.

But almost any activity can be improved with just a little thought and some extra effort. Change is indispensable to progress and progress comes only with change.

Change always starts with an idea. Here are some methods Chris Ireland, Director of Dow Chemical's Special Projects Division, says you can use to change the status quo and revamp your present system so you can go for the maximum.

"**Re-examine your thinking.** Repress old ideas and solutions; push the accepted methods aside temporarily while you look for new methods. Examine new ideas with the uninhibited curiosity of a child. Develop the knack of seeing things as if you were seeing them for the very first time.

"**Do some brainstorming with other people.** Probe the minds of others. Use questions to stimulate thinking. The method here is to suspend critical judgment while suggesting new ideas. There's plenty of time for evaluation later. Now you want as many new ideas as possible. So no matter how crazy a method sounds, jot it down. You must create a freewheeling atmosphere to get the most out of brainstorming.

"**Keep your imagination turned on all the time.** Don't turn your brain off when you go home from work. Fresh ideas can pop up all the time, during conversation with a friend—while reading a magazine or newspaper—walking, shaving, showering, eating. You can force your mind to work all the time if you will. Keep a notebook handy. You never know when that idea is going to come and you don't want to miss it.

"**Be willing to accept new ideas.**   It's easy to come up with all sorts of reasons why something new won't work. If you want your people to do their best to come up with new ideas and ways of doing things, then you must keep an open mind. You must be willing to give their ideas a fair try."

Whenever you arbitrarily push a new idea to the side, you're hammering another nail into the coffin of a dying organization. You can't get the maximum out of people that way. Any company that refuses to accept new methods or even to listen to new ideas is not growing—it's not even standing still. In fact, it's not only going backward—it's dying.

Encourage Your Employees to Better Your System

"Wage incentive plans are used quite extensively in many industries today," says Richard Ellis, Production Superintendent for the American Smelting and Refining Company in Wallace, Idaho. "The method is to set a production quota and establish a certain standard of performance. Then you challenge your employees to beat your system and produce more so they can earn more incentive pay.

"You can motivate a person to give his maximum when you challenge him to beat a system you've established. You tax his ingenuity and his initiative. Of course, when he succeeds, you must keep your end of the bargain and reward him with money and praise, possibly promotion."

Most managers can use this method successfully in production and sales where they're challenging their employees to *beat* the system. But they fail to use it properly in what they look at as the nonproductive parts of their business such as office and clerical help, secretarial services, accounting, bookkeeping, warehousing, maintenance, etc., for there the employee normally has no opportunity to *beat* the system, but only to *better* it.

For example, suppose your present office filing system is not satisfactory. It takes far too long for your people to locate records, correspondence, and the like. Don't try to change it yourself. Have your clerks, your secretaries, your office personnel come up with suggestions on improvement. Let them figure out how to *better* your system. Then reward them the same way you would your production line employees or your sales people: with money, praise, and promotion.

Or suppose your warehouse foreman comes up with some new ways to store your goods that cut down on warehouse space and product spoilage. Your shipping department supervisor has figured out a way to load trucks that cuts their dock time by a fourth. Your maintenance foreman shows you how he can service the plant machinery without stopping or even slowing down your production lines.

Aren't these people entitled to something, too? If you reward them properly, if you don't place all your emphasis on production and sales alone, these people in your service departments will give you their maximum, too. And they'll do their best to *better* your present system.

Help People to Set Goals for Themselves

A lot of people just seem to drift along in a never-never land. They have some vague and indefinite ideas about what they want out of life, but they never seem to be able to come up with any concrete and specific plans to get it.

In his book, *How I Raised Myself from Failure to Success in Selling,** Frank Bettger says, in effect, that "the most important secret of salesmanship is to find out what people want, and to help them get it."

Mr. Bettger's statement is as applicable to management as it is to salesmanship. One of the best ways I know of to get the maximum out of a person is to *help him determine what he wants most out of life and then show him how to get it.*

To make a person goal-minded on the job so he'll give his maximum for you, use these six techniques:

1. **Make his goal specific.** To get your employee out of that vague dream world, make him get specific about what he wants from you. For instance, is he aiming for more money— financial security? Is he interested in a better job or promotion? Does he have his sights set on a certain position in the company?

---

* Frank Bettger, *How I Raised Myself from Failure to Success in Selling,* (Englewood Cliffs, New Jersey: Prentice-Hall, 1949).

Do anything and everything you can to help him make his goal specific and concrete.

2. Help him develop a plan for achieving his goal.   Show him what he has to do to attain his goal. If more education or training is required, tell him exactly what will be needed. Have him get his plan down in writing; it will help him know whether he really wants to put out that extra effort or not.

3. Make his goal exciting and worthwhile.   Help him see how he'll benefit when he reaches his goal. Kindle his desire for success by enumerating the material rewards and psychic benefits that will be his. Remember that *desire is the first law of gain.* A man must want to succeed before he ever will.

4. Let him compete with himself.   When a man fails to beat his own record, he can take it a lot better than when he's defeated by someone else. His foe can be a quota or a record he wants to break—a standard he wants to improve—a new time he wants to establish—any impersonal target other than a human being.

5. Make his goal attainable.   Be sure his goal is realistic, reasonable, and attainable. To have a man with an eighth-grade education make his goal a position that requires a Ph.D. in chemistry would be extremely unwise. Yet people many times do give themselves an impossible goal and then give up completely when they don't make it.

6. Reward him when he succeeds.   Don't promise a man a reward unless you can fulfill your promises when he does succeed. As Elmer Wheeler would say, "Don't sell a man an empty box." *

Make a Man Proud of His Job

No matter what his job is, every person wants to take pride in what he does. The desire for praise, attention, and approval is one of the most powerful incentives to which nearly every single person will respond.

I am proud of you is one of the most potent sentences you can ever use to get a man to go all out for you. So use it.

---

* Elmer Wheeler, *How to Sell Yourself to Others* (Englewood Cliffs, New Jersey: Prentice-Hall, 1947).

And remember this, too: *Unless a man is proud of himself, his job, and his organization, you cannot possibly get the maximum from him.* It just can't be done.

One of the dirtiest, most miserable jobs I have ever seen a man do was that of a scaler in one of our West Coast shipyards back in World War II. A scaler's job was to chip all the rust off steel plates on prefabricated sections used in ship construction. He worked in a confined double bottom, in a space only three feet wide between the walls. The noise from his tools was absolutely deafening. Red dust filled the air he breathed and choked him. The blazing sun beat down on the steel plates above him and raised the temperature to well over 100 degrees.

The scalers complained bitterly about their working conditions and their low pay scale—for their job was classed as unskilled labor—but management refused to listen to their complaints. The scalers did not actually strike, but they slowed down their work so much that the shipyard soon fell behind schedule in its production.

Then one young scaler was made foreman over several hundred workers and given the task of getting things straightened out and back to normal. It was a job many more experienced foremen had turned down flat. Immediately the new foreman began visiting his men. He listened with patient attention to their gripes. He lent a sympathetic ear to the scalers, agreeing with them that they were doing the dirtiest, the unhealthiest, the most unwanted, and the most underpaid job in the shipyard.

"But your job has to be done, too," he told them. "Without you the ships couldn't be built. The rust has to be removed. And there's just no other way to do it. But remember this: wherever you go in this shipyard, the other employees see the scaler buttons you wear. They know you have what it takes and then some. They also know they don't have the guts to do what you're doing. *You can be proud to be a scaler.*"

With renewed pride in their work, the scalers gave up their slowdown and went back to work. But now they carried their heads higher and stuck out their chests as never before. And all because a young foreman realized a man's work had to be important to him before he would give the job everything he had to give. *When he gave them the pride they needed, they gave him the best they had to give—their maximum performance.*

There are other techniques you can use to go for the maximum instead of just placidly accepting the minimum. For instance, you can throw down a challenge; you can give your people a cause to fight for; you can set up tests for maximum potential by giving a man a bigger job to do; you can give your people the opportunity to tell you how they need to improve. I'm sure you can think of many, many more.

Watch for These Tell-Tale Signs of Minimum Performance

To wrap up this chapter, I want to let you know how to detect the signs and symptoms of minimum performance in your organization. If you find any of the following, you're not getting the maximum out of your people:

1. Management is no longer willing to experiment, to take chances, or to try new methods or new ideas.
2. The company is no longer looking for new markets and new customers, but is satisfied to hold what it has.
3. The organization demands absolute conformity from its employees. It attracts only passive and dependent people to its work force.
4. Promotion is based on seniority—not on performance.
5. Management is self-satisfied. It no longer has a program of self-development and self-improvement.
6. The organization is a boring place to work; it is dull, lifeless, and presents no challenge whatever.

TEN

Using Your Management Position for Personal Gain

Frank McGee, the popular NBC newscaster who replaced Hugh Downs as host of the "Today" show, once said, "When all other human motives fail, you can always depend on greed."

You can read about people like this in your newspaper nearly every day of the week, people in exceptionally high places who let their greed get the best of them and used their positions for personal gain: big city mayors, labor union leaders, businessmen, industrialists, senators, congressmen, military officers, even ministers.

One such person who comes to my mind immediately, probably because his position called for a person of high moral standards and integrity, is Carl Turner, at one time a two star major general and the Provost Marshal of the United States Army.

Major General Turner was the army's top policeman. His position as Provost Marshal General was comparable to that of the Chief of the FBI. General Turner had the responsibility of maintaining law, order, and discipline in the entire United States Army, both at home and abroad.

But General Turner did not set a personal example for his officers and soldiers to follow. In fact, he used his high-ranking position of trust, not to serve, but for personal gain. This was discovered when he testified before the Senate's Permanent Investigating Committee that he had accepted a large number of confiscated guns from the chiefs of police of Chicago and Kansas City.

"I accepted these guns only after I made it clear to both police chiefs that they were for my own personal use," General Turner said.

But the Senate Subcommittee didn't believe the general. His story did not sound at all reasonable so their chief investigator, a lawyer named La Verne Duffy, immediately called the two police chiefs on the telephone to hear their versions of the transaction.

"General Turner told us the guns were for training purposes and museum use in the army," they said. "He never once even intimated that they were for his own personal use. Had he said that, we'd never have given the guns to him."

So the next morning, General Turner and the two police chiefs sat side by side at the same witness stand to testify before the Senate Subcommittee. They all repeated the same statements under oath.

Of course, it was obvious that someone was lying under oath to a Senate Subcommittee, and that's a federal offense. The transcript of the hearing was turned over to the Justice Department for complete investigation and possible prosecution. Soon after, General Turner, in effect, conceded that the police chiefs were telling the truth. He was found guilty without the need for a trial.

The general had used his high position of public trust for personal gain for *he had sold the guns he'd obtained under false pretenses for several thousand dollars.* He lost his general's rank and went to jail for income tax evasion and a variety of other charges.

I could give you dozens of other examples of people who used their high positions for personal gain, but that's not my purpose in this section. My aim is to show you some positive techniques you can use to gain the . . .

BENEFITS THAT WILL BE YOURS
WHEN YOU DON'T USE YOUR MANAGEMENT
POSITION FOR PERSONAL GAIN

You Can Live with Yourself

"Not that I'm any paragon of virtue; I'm not," says Robert L. Edwards, National Sales Director for the Monsanto Chemical Company. "But I can honestly say I've never used an executive or management position for personal gain. I've never had to worry about an auditor going over my records or checking my cash funds, or a security guard opening my briefcase or the trunk of my car, anything like that. And I can sleep without the help of sleeping pills. I take no tranquilizers of any sort. I can live with myself."

Your Employees Will Trust You

When your people know you're not using your management position for personal gain at their expense, they'll trust you and have confidence in you. You'll gain their loyalty and their whole-hearted support.

"A credibility gap has become extremely common today, not only in government, but also in big business and industry, between the leaders and their people," says Jay Dalton, Chief Purchasing Agent for the Bendix Corporation of Kansas City. "A person who tells it like it is, no matter what the consequences to himself, or who isn't trying to milk some special privileges and advantages out of his position—especially at the expense of his own subordinates—will be highly regarded by his employees."

With just a little effort on your part, you can be that person.

You'll Gain Your Employees' Admiration and Respect

When your employees see that you're not abusing the privileges of your position, you'll gain their admiration and respect. And when they also realize you're more concerned about their personal welfare and well-being on the job than you are with your own, they'll develop a positive attitude toward you that will be most helpful to you in gaining their willing obedience, their confidence, and their whole-hearted support.

In fact, if you play it clean and straight with your subordinates, you'll come on like a breath of fresh air. Not only will they respect you and admire you, but they'll also go so far as to like you!

You'll Pull Your Employees Up to Your Level

Employees tend to imitate the boss and pick up his mannerisms. They are inclined always to do as their superior does —to follow his example.

By not using your management position for personal gain, you'll find your subordinates will emulate you. Honesty will increase; petty thievery will decrease. Your own integrity on the job will set a positive example for them to follow. By your actions alone, you can motivate and inspire people to pull themselves up to your high standards.

TECHNIQUES YOU CAN USE TO GAIN THESE BENEFITS

Use Your Managerial Resources for their Intended Purposes

If you'll recall, back in Chapter Seven I said that every manager has five resources at his disposal to get the job done. These resources are people, money, materials, time, and facilities.

Whenever you divert any of these resources from their original intended use by your company to your own private benefit, you're using your management position for personal gain. Let me give you a quick simple example to illustrate this idea.

Suppose you dictate a private letter to your company-paid secretary that will be typed on a company letter-head, sealed in a company envelope, and mailed with a company stamp. By this one simple act, you've abused your privileges and misused all five of your managerial resources:

1. *People.* You've used your secretary, who's employed and paid by the company, to do a personal service for you. And though it might not have occurred to you before, you've also misused yourself. After all, you're being paid by the company, too.

2. *Money.* The company pays both you and your secretary to do company work, but you've used that money to do your own personal work.

3. *Materials.* Your letter was typed on company stationery, sealed in a company envelope, mailed with a company stamp.

4. *Time.* Both your time and your secretary's time belong to the company during working hours. But you used that time for your personal work.

5. *Facilities.* Your personal letter was typed on a company typewriter in the company office using company desks, chairs, lights, heat, etc.

This is an extremely small example of how managerial resources can be diverted from their original intended purpose. You might feel it's quite minor and unimportant because it's so small and perhaps so commonplace. Could be it's only a tiny leak in the dam, but once the water starts to flow, it's hard to stop.

Practice the Old-Fashioned Virtue of Honesty

The moment you're guilty of any dishonesty, no matter how slight—whenever you take anything at all for your own personal use without paying for it, no matter how small—you've weakened your moral authority over your subordinates. Your employees will criticize, ridicule, despise you. You'll never be able to regain their complete respect.

You should never accept any material favors from your employees. Oh, you'll get all kinds of offers if you're the boss or in any position of authority. Those offers will range from shirts and pants, meats and cheeses, to tools and office supplies. It all depends on what the company makes or what the employee can scrounge for you. But if you'll take my advice, you won't take anything—period.

"A lot of times you'll take the item without even thinking about it and then pay the penalty later," says Merle Nichols, Director of Safety and Loss Prevention for the Puget Sound Naval Shipyard in Bremerton, Washington.

"For instance, the second morning after I took over this job, the chief storekeeper came by and wanted to know my shoe size," Mr. Nichols says. "When I came back from lunch that afternoon, I found a brand-new pair of expensive safety shoes on my desk.

"Well, I was busy learning a new job so I stuck them down in a desk drawer and forgot all about them. About a week later my secretary stuck her head in the door and said, 'The chief storekeeper, Mr. Hobbs, would like to see you.'

"Mr. Hobbs came in, sat down without being asked to do so, leisurely lighted up a cigarette, smiled expansively at me, and said, 'How are your new shoes? Do they fit you all right? Is there anything else you need?'

"As I looked at Mr. Hobbs, his face seemed to assume the features of a larcenous old army supply sergeant who'd got to me when I was a young and green inexperienced second lieutenant.

"When I took command of my first training company at Fort Ord, he'd loaded my desk down with fatigue uniforms, combat boots, field jackets, blankets, sheets, all those expensive but necessary items young second lieutenants have no money for.

"Like a fool I took everything he had to offer. And for the next six months he had me in his pocket. He had me right where he wanted me. I made the mistake of thinking all officers took such extra privileges. I found out they did not.

"And remembering that experience and not wanting to repeat it, I said to Mr. Hobbs, 'How much do these safety shoes cost?'

" 'To you, nothing,' he said. 'Consider them a gift.'

" 'But who paid for them?'

" 'The company,' he said. 'But that's all right. I'm entitled to a small operating loss to cover things like this.'

" 'Do other employees here in the shipyard pay for them?'

" 'Oh yes,' he said. 'They cost them $38.75 a pair, but after all, you're the safety director so there's no cost to you.'

" 'Do I have to have them?' I asked.

" 'Of course,' he said. 'You must always wear them out in the work area.'

" 'Then prepare the proper bill for them,' I said, 'or take them back, and I'll buy a pair somewhere else. I will not accept them as a gift.' "

You should refuse such gifts from your subordinates just as Mr. Nichols did. There are too many strings attached and you certainly don't want to be the puppet dangling from the end of them.

You Must Follow the Rules, Too

Sometimes managers tend to forget that the rules are for them to follow, too. Safety rules are often violated by managers when they're inspecting the actual physical work.

One that always rubs an employee raw is to see a foreman or a supervisor smoking a cigarette in a no-smoking area when no one else is allowed to do so.

And speaking of smoking reminds me of an incident a friend of mine told me about the other day.

"I'd found some marijuana in my son's jacket pocket," Jack said, "and I was giving him a lecture about why he shouldn't be using it, like how we don't know enough about its effects on the mind or the body, and how it could possibly lead to the use of hard drugs. I ended up by saying whether it was harmful or not was beside the point, for after all, the use of marijuana was strictly against the law.

"But Doug really stopped me cold when he said, 'So was cheating on your income tax last year when you claimed Mary as a dependent even though she got married the year before. But that was different, Dad, wasn't it!' "

So you see, you must follow the rules, too. It isn't enough to tell your people to do as you tell them to do. They won't listen to you, especially if your actions are different than your words. They'll do as you do or as they want to do.

Give Credit to Your Subordinates for the Work They Do

To take for yourself credit that really belongs to one of your people tends to destroy that person's initiative, his willingness to take on responsibility, and his usefulness to you. On the other hand, giving him fair recognition for what he does has a dual beneficial effect. He gets appreciation for doing a good job and you win the willing cooperation of a loyal worker who will support both you and the company.

Just for instance, say you ask one of your assistants to stay on the job late at night to finish up a project ahead of time that'll make you look good. Don't take all the credit the next day for getting the job done. At least share the limelight with him; give him credit for what he's done, too.

"I'm always highly suspicious of progress reports, office memos, or correspondence that say *'We* accomplished this; *we* did that,'" says Samuel Horowitz, executive vice-president of Feinberg and Lowenstein, a New York garment manufacturing firm.

"When I do a little probing beneath the surface, I usually find that the signer of the letter actually contributed very little, perhaps even nothing, to it. It's just a slick way of grabbing some of the credit for something someone else has done. I don't get fooled too often by managers of this kind. I can usually smell one out by the way he does his paper work."

So make sure to give credit to your subordinates for the work they do. If your department is to be commended for outstanding efforts or for some worthwhile achievement, then pass the proper credit along to those people v'ho've made this accomplishment possible for you. You'll benefit by having employees who'll work that much harder for you.

How to Develop the Character Trait of Unselfishness

The selfish manager will provide for his own comfort and his own personal advancement *even at the expense of his own subordinates.*

But as an unselfish manager, you must learn to place the welfare of your subordinates above your own. You should never try to gain your own ends at their expense. You must remember to practice the precept that he who would be the greatest of all must first be the servant of all.

Here are a couple of ways you can do that:

1. Be concerned about your employee's working conditions. "If you are not concerned about your employee's working conditions, if you neglect his health and welfare on the job, you're hurting yourself, too," says Lloyd Harrison, publisher of the *Cleveland Daily Tribune*. "To promote good working conditions for your people is good business for you'll benefit in the long run, too. You'll reap dividends for yourself by making every person in your plant as effective as possible in his work for you."

Just remember that the skilled employee who stays at home sick in bed because of an injury he suffered while working in your plant is costing you time, money, and loss of quality production. Not only that, you're probably paying premium overtime pay to the man who's taking his place.

2. Don't abuse your privileges. None of your subordinates will object to the extra privileges that go with your office as long as you use your position to guard and protect their interests, too. But they will object strenuously when you assume privileges that are not rightfully and legitimately yours.

For instance, the army officer who uses government transportation to get from his home to his work, or eats in a company mess hall without paying for it, or uses an enlisted man as a personal servant, is despised by all his men. So is the traveling salesman who pads his expense account, or the plant manager who uses company materials and company labor for his own private benefit.

Don't abuse your privileges that way. If you're an executive or a manager, a foreman or a supervisor, a leader of any sort—play your part to the letter. Your subordinates will expect you to. But they'll never take exception to your title, your position, your prerogatives, or your privileges as long as you don't abuse them and as long as you use your position to protect their interests and to help them get what they want.

Let me wrap up this chapter by saying that to think of your management position as one that offers you only reward and privilege is wrong. Positions of management are created to serve, not just as a reward to the person filling that position.

Certainly, executive and management privileges do go along with your job, but so does the responsibility of serving people, and *service is far more important than status.*

Your management position was created to allow you to fulfill your responsibility to your superiors by serving your subordinates. If you think of it that way, you can't possibly go wrong.

ELEVEN

Failing to Tell the Truth—To Always Keep Your Word

The other day I read an article called "Ten Commandments for Executives and Managers." It said to be an effective executive or manager, you must gain the respect of your people . . . be a good listener . . . help people solve their problems . . . practice the Golden Rule . . . control your temper . . . know how to motivate people . . . be willing to go the extra mile . . . know each person individually . . . forgive and forget.

Nowhere did I find a commandment to tell the truth—to always keep your word. Nor did I find that idea even mentioned anywhere in that article.

A little later on I read another article entitled "Twenty-Five Ways to Recognize the Perfect Supervisor." Just a few of the ways mentioned were that a good supervisor makes his people want to do things, pinpoints priorities, plays up the positive, follows up and follows through, helps his people grow, avoids domination, is receptive to new ideas, etc.

Again, nowhere did I find even the barest mention of the fact that to be a perfect supervisor you would have to keep your word—you would always need to tell the truth.

My curiosity was aroused. I read more articles, scanned a dozen excellent books on leadership, supervision, management, executive development. But nowhere did I once find that *telling the truth and keeping your word* was considered important by any of the authors. None of them even once mentioned the idea.

And I thought, *Am I getting old-fashioned? Am I com-*

pletely out of date? I'd always felt that telling the truth or keeping my promise was absolutely fundamental in my relationships with others. In fact, I can still remember my father's lecture to me when I made the mistake of lying to him for the first and only time.

"The most important attribute a man can have is character, son," he said to me. "Without character, a man is nothing. A man of character is always able to know right from wrong and he will have the courage to adhere to the right. He is a man of honor . . . a man to be trusted . . . a man of his word. He does not lie, cheat, or steal. He does not chisel. He is a person of good repute. No man can climb above the limitations of his own character. Remember that."

But evidently the people who'd written all those well worthwhile articles and books on leadership, supervision, management, and executive development assumed that everyone was so honest and truthful that they saw no reason to stress the necessity of developing this character trait.

If that is true, I asked myself, why is there such a credibility gap between government leaders and the people? Why do we consider a politician's solemn pledges as little more than a bunch of "campaign promises," or worse yet, outright lies? Why is there such a deep distrust of government agencies, corporations, manufacturers, warranties and guarantees, packaging, advertising claims? Why do we need people like Ralph Nader and Bess Myerson? Why does the consumer need to be protected?

My conclusion was simply this: to keep your word—to tell the truth at all times might not always be popular, but it's still highly important.

So at the risk of being old-fashioned and out of date or sounding like Horatio Alger, I decided to include this chapter in my book. If you feel you don't need it, fine: congratulations. But if you decide to read it, here are some of the . . .

BENEFITS YOU'LL GAIN

People Will Believe What You Say

When you gain the reputation of telling the truth and always keeping your word, people will believe what you say and they'll do what you ask them to do, knowing it's the right thing.

But if you're a liar, you simply cannot be depended on. You could be a genius, but as a manager or a leader you'd be completely worthless. So unless you do tell the truth, you might as well forget about trying to get along with your boss or motivate your employees to do their best for you.

You'll Gain the Reputation of Being Dependable

When you are dependable—when your performance of duty can always be relied on with absolute certainty by your boss—he will depend on you more and more to get the job done for him. He knows he can trust you.

You can enhance your reputation for reliability by complying willingly with the plans and desires of your superior. This does not mean that you should give him your blind obedience. But it does mean that you can be relied upon to give him your complete and energetic support at all times.

You'll Be Respected by Everyone

A man who tells the truth, who keeps his word, who never breaks his promises, is respected by everyone. You can have a lot of other faults that people will forgive you for as long as they know you are telling them the truth. It's terribly difficult to criticize a man or to be angry with him when he admits he's wrong and accepts the blame without question when he's at fault. Such a man is always highly respected by others. Always tell the truth and keep your word so you can be that man.

You Won't Have to Remember What You Say

At first glance, this might not seem like much of a benefit to you, but it's truly a big one. People who cannot be depended on to tell the truth are constantly in a dither trying to remember what they said to whom. Tell the truth and you won't have to memorize what you said. You'll have a lot more time and energy to concentrate on your own job.

TECHNIQUES YOU CAN USE TO GAIN THESE BENEFITS

Develop Moral Courage

"Physical bravery begins in the mind—not in the muscles," says Colonel Robert L. Green, a much-decorated infantry combat veteran of three wars. "Courage is first of all a mental quality—an attitude—a state of mind. If a man is courageous, he will recognize his fear of danger or criticism, but he will control that fear.

"Courage is not necessarily the absence of fear, as so many people think. *Courage is the control of fear.* When a man is able to control his fears, he'll be able to control himself and his own actions. His self-control enables him to accept responsibility and to conduct himself properly even in a dangerous combat situation. His moral courage is vital to military leadership."

Moral courage is needed off the battlefield by us civilians, too. You need it in your job as a manager. When you have moral courage, you will be able to stand up for what you know to be right, to do the right thing regardless of the consequences, and to accept the blame when you are wrong. Your people will respect you when you have such strong moral courage as this, and that's a good thing.

Never Make a Promise You Cannot Keep

If you're going to be a top-notch manager, you must be as good as your word and your word must be your bond. Never make a promise you cannot keep or announce a punishment for a certain act and then not carry through on it. If you don't intend to keep your promises, don't make them. If you're not going to punish a man, don't say you are. You only make things worse for yourself with empty promises or idle threats.

"Many times a foreman or a supervisor will make false promises to his people to get results, all the while knowing he can't possibly fulfill those promises," says Dallas Collins, Director of Industrial Relations for Midland Steel in Gary, Indiana. "My job here is to keep peace between labor and management. My door is always open to anyone who feels he has a gripe or that he's been treated unfairly.

"Most beefs are about money. For instance, last week a man came to me and said, 'My last foreman told me I was doing good work and that if I kept it up, he'd promote me to senior supervisor on the day shift in January with a good pay increase. He's gone, it's February, I'm still on the night shift, and I didn't get the promotion or the raise.'

"The best I could do in this case was apologize and have the new foreman listen to his story. Then I told the foreman —in front of the supervisor—to keep his eye on him, and if he did prove worthy of promotion to let me know and I'd take care of it.

"I always advise all our management personnel not to promise a man something that's beyond their authority to take care of. That causes nothing but distrust and hard feelings when they do. Trouble is, they don't always listen."

I've seen the same thing happen and I'm sure you have, too. In fact, maybe it's happened to you; I know it's happened to me. I've heard managers at all levels make all sorts of promises to their subordinates of more money, promotion, extra time off, and then when the job's done, they forget everything they've promised their men.

You can't get the results you want that way. Maybe you can the first time, and possibly the second time, but no more than that. Even the most loyal employee you have won't go for that line of yours the third time.

So don't try it that way. Never make a promise you cannot keep and never renege on a promised reward. If you know you can't live up to your promises, don't make them.

Always Carry Through with Announced Punishment

The same thing can be said for punishment. If you tell a man what the punishment is going to be for doing a certain thing and then fail to punish him when he does it, you might as well throw in the towel before you climb into the ring. You'll never become a top-level manager that way.

This idea applies to your children, too. If you tell your son he's going to lose his weekly allowance the next time he stays out until two in the morning and then fail to make it stick, you're no longer the boss—he is.

Your employees are no different; they'll try to test you,

too, to see how much they can get by with. If you use only empty threats, they'll know they're the boss—not you. You might occupy the position, but you're not really filling it.

How to Be Thought Of As Being Dependable

If you always tell the truth and keep your word, if you continually put forth your best efforts to achieve the highest possible standards of performance, you'll be thought of as a reliable individual, a person who can be depended on at all times. To develop this kind of dependability,

Do every job to the best of your ability. No matter whether the task you've been given is big or small, interesting or dull, important or seemingly unimportant to you, do it to the best of your ability.

Last summer I visited the John F. Kennedy Space Center and took the NASA tour. One of the buildings we visited was the blockhouse used for the first manned mission control center. Everything was still in place: the desks, chairs, computers, television monitors, and all the complicated scientific equipment required for that launch. When I thought of the detailed work it took to complete that mission, my mind boggled and refused to comprehend it.

So be exact in the details; they are important. Nothing can be done except little by little. And if you can't be depended on to do those little things, your boss will hesitate to trust you with bigger ones.

The rules are for you to follow, too. If you expect your people to be on time, you should be on time yourself. In fact, you should be the first one in the place. And if you want them to work overtime, you ought to be the last one out. You might not punch the clock, literally speaking, but the point is, do as you expect your people to do—not just as you tell them to do. The rules are for you to follow, too.

Carry out the spirit of the order. If you do what you have to do grudgingly and with resentment, your subordinates will do their work the same way. If you disagree with the order you've been given, get a clarification from your boss. Once you've got it, stop grumbling. Accept his answer with courtesy and good grace. Be cheerful and optimistic. To whistle while you work isn't nearly as Pollyannish as it might sound to you at first.

How to Develop the Character Trait of Integrity

If you are going to tell the truth and always keep your word, you must develop the character trait of personal integrity. Integrity, the uprightness of character and soundness of moral principles, the quality of absolute truthfulness and honesty, is an indispensable trait of a manager, an executive, a supervisor, a leader of any kind.

Unless you are honest, you cannot be relied upon at all. There is absolutely no compromise whatever. Never allow yourself the slightest deviation from the highest standards of personal integrity. To develop personal integrity—

Practice absolute honesty and truthfulness at all times. Don't allow yourself the luxury of even one tiny white lie. I can think of no exception to this rule whatsoever. Of course, this doesn't mean that you are to insult a person or hurt his feelings. If you can say nothing good about him, then do just that: say nothing.

Be accurate and truthful in all your statements. This includes statements both oral and written—official and unofficial. Your signature on any document, any correspondence, any piece of paper is your certification that the information is correct.

When you sign a personal check, your signature is your certificate that you have enough money in the bank to cover that check. Your signature in your work and on the job must carry the same weight.

"In my experiences I've found that most managers are reluctant to sign their names to a subordinate's performance report if it contains unfavorable comments," says Donald Ryan, Personnel Manager for the General Dynamics Corporation of Houston, Texas.

"They also hesitate to call a subordinate in for a discussion of his faults face to face. They are reluctant to report serious violations of rules and regulations—even those that involved dereliction of duty. Time after time I've seen them cover up for a man who drinks too much. I think they fail to realize that to lie for such a man, to allow him to be promoted, is an injustice, not only to the company and to the man, but also to themselves."

No doubt you, too, will be called upon to face similar situations periodically, perhaps even daily, in your relationships with others. How you react will depend upon how well you have developed your character trait of personal integrity.

Stand for what you believe to be right. Have the courage of your convictions. Never compromise your high moral standards; never prostitute your principles.

A great many times, one man's courageous stand can save the day. One man's courage and integrity in a situation where a tough decision is required can point the right way for an entire group.

Some time ago I attended a retirement function in Des Moines, Iowa, for a high-ranking executive of the Banker's Life Company. The president of the company paid him this final tribute:

"Jack has been with our company for many years," he said. "In all that time, I have never seen him fail to stand for what he believed to be right. Whenever there was a tough decision to be made that required integrity and courage, Jack always faced the issue squarely, no matter how unpleasant or unpopular it was. He always insisted that we make the *right* decision and he gave the rest of us the courage we needed to make it."

Accept the blame when you are wrong. This, too, takes a high standard of personal integrity. Not only does a man have the tendency to pass the buck, but a great many times he'll even lie to you to get out from under. But to lie will only make things worse. One lie leads to another and yet another, and you'll soon find yourself entangled in a web of falsehoods if you attempt that route.

The best thing to do is accept the blame when you're at fault. When you goof, admit it. Don't try to rationalize away your mistakes, look for scapegoats, or sulk.

One of my main gripes about the army is its unwillingness to live and let live, especially in the lower ranks. It always has to find a culprit—that's the order of the day—and it never gives up until it does. If only it had such admirable tenacity when it comes to more important matters.

No one will expect you to be infallible. Just admit it when you're wrong. Your people will gain confidence in you because of your honesty.

To sum it up, let me say that if you ever are tempted to compromise (and I'm sure you will be), then place honor, your sense of duty, and moral principles above all else. Doing that, you cannot possibly fail.

TWELVE

Not Setting the Personal Example for Your People to Follow

Being a writer brings me all sorts of unique fringe benefits —benefits I would not otherwise be able to enjoy. For instance, I'm often invited by the president or general manager of some company to come behind the scenes with him to see what really goes on.

And so I've been lucky enough to see the internal operations of big department stores . . . large factories . . . automobile assembly plants . . . airports . . . shipyards . . . television and radio stations . . . newspaper and magazine editorial offices. Such intimate visits are both fascinating and profitable, for they give me a wealth of material to draw from for my writing. Sometimes I can even help them a little bit, too.

Like several months ago George Orr, Manager of the Dayton Rubber and Tire Company's Springday plant, took me on a tour of his place. He wanted me to see some projects that'd been added and look at some new equipment he'd installed since my last visit. As we walked through the various departments, I saw several things George didn't point out to me.

I saw a foreman jump up on a guard rail and leap over a running conveyor belt despite a warning sign not to do so. A young chemist—a junior executive from the research department, George said—was supervising some experimental work at a mixing mill. He wore no face mask to filter out the powder and carbon black that filled the air, nor did he have on the required plant-approved safety shoes. He also wore a four-in-hand tie that was strictly forbidden when doing mixing mill work, according to the big safety poster on the wall directly over the mill. I saw a young accountant from the controller's department hitching a ride on the front of an electric fork lift by standing on one of the blades. This is strictly forbidden in any plant I've ever been in.

Then I saw a supervisor enter a section of the plant where new construction was going on. He failed to stop and put on a hard hat, although he passed right by a dozen of them on a table that'd been especially put there for people entering that area. I knew he should've put one on, for a sign mounted on an A-frame in front of the table read: ALL PERSONNEL STOP HERE. PUT ON HARD HAT BEFORE ENTERING CONSTRUCTION AREA.

After we were back in his office, George said, "Well, what do you think of the operation?"

"I think you have a high accident rate," I said.

George frowned and said, "We do have, but how did you know?"

I told him what I'd seen, and then, since we've known each other a long time, I risked our friendship by saying, "And I'll bet your production is off—both in quality and quantity. You're probably running a high rejection rate in your quality control section, maybe even getting a lot of customer complaints about your product."

"You're right," George said. "To tell the truth, the main office in Chicago is on my back all the time. What would you recommend?"

"This is right off the top of my head," I said, "and I'd much rather have a couple of weeks to go over your whole set-up in detail, but from what little I've seen this morning I'd say your management people aren't setting the example for your employees to follow.

"Evidently they feel the rules don't apply to them, for I've seen safety regulations violated all over the place this morning. And if they're careless about safety, then your employees will be careless, too—not just about safety rules—but about everything. Get your management people to set the personal example for their men to follow, George, and see if things don't improve for you."

Last week George called me. "You were right," he said. "Things are improving. Production is up; accident rate is down; customer complaints are fewer. Better make setting an example for others to follow a chapter in your new book, Jim." So I did. I figured if it helped George that much, it'd help you, too.

Now, besides the *advantages of better production, fewer customer complaints, and lower accident rate* George achieved by getting his management people to *use the technique of following the rules themselves to set the example for their people fo follow*, here are some more . . .

BENEFITS YOU'LL GAIN BY SETTING THE EXAMPLE FOR YOUR PEOPLE TO FOLLOW

Your People Will Come Up to Your Standards

When you set the personal example for others to follow, you'll inspire them and motivate them to do as you do. Everyone tends to do as his superior does. Set the proper example for them to follow so they will come up to your standards. How high you want to set those standards depends entirely on you.

You'll Get the Best Out of Your People

To gain the respect, confidence, willing obedience, loyal cooperation, and full support of your employees, you must set the example for them to follow by giving the best you're capable of. You'll never go wrong if you follow the advice of General Robert E. Lee, the South's great hero of more than a hundred years ago. "Do your duty in all things," he said. "You could not do more; you should not wish to do less." Time has not dimmed the wisdom of his remarks; it never will.

TECHNIQUES YOU CAN USE TO GAIN THE BENEFITS

Set a High Standard for Them to Follow

"I myself must set the standard in all things for my employees to follow," says Carl Vance, manager of one of the biggest Montgomery Ward stores I've ever seen in Dallas, Texas. "And confidence in the successful completion of a difficult job or the achievement of a specific sales goal is one of the most important ways that I, as a manager, can set that example.

"By my every act and word I must show my own confidence in the successful outcome of a tough project. If I show the least bit of doubt, I'll most certainly cause my people to have doubts of their own. Success, then, is not likely to follow. So setting the standard of confidence is an important part of my job as a manager. I'm sure it's an important part of yours, too."

This same idea applies to many other relationships with your people, too. For instance, you'll want them to be courteous, respectful, loyal, and cooperative. So you must set the standard yourself by showing them courtesy, respect, and loyalty, and by cooperating with them first. You must lead the way.

If you are irregular in your own work habits, late for your appointments, careless about safety rules, apparently bored with your own work, the people under you will act the same way. On the other hand, if you're punctual in coming to work and on time for your appointments, if you obey the safety rules, if you're enthusiastic about your work, if you set a high standard by your own stellar performance of duty, they'll be eager and anxious to follow your good example.

Remember that any organization is an accurate mirror of the viewpoints, strengths, confidences, fears, and shortcomings of its leader. It is inescapable that you must set the standard and the example in all things. It can be no other way.

Set the Example by Working Hard

"One of the best ways to set the example is to work hard yourself," says Tedd Hoffman, Safety Director for the Budd Company of Philadelphia. "Few things will command more attention than plain, old-fashioned hard work. Stop thinking about what you can get out of your job and concentrate on what you can put in it for a change.

"Put out some extra effort. Skip your coffee break or have your secretary bring it to your desk once in a while. Shorten your lunch hour. Come to work early some of the time. Stay until your desk is clear at night. Be willing to go beyond the call of duty—to go the extra mile. Try that for just one month. Your efficiency on the job will skyrocket. And let me tell you this, too. The man who works hard—every day of the week and every hour of the day when he's on the job—is still rare enough to stand out in any group."

Mr. Hoffman gives you a clue about *how* to work hard in his last sentence, and that is to—

Make every minute count while you're on the job. Don't have any lost motion; don't make any false moves. Never read the same piece of paper twice. Avoid telephone traps. Stay away from the crowd at the water fountain; don't waste time in idle gossip.

Be friendly to visitors, of course, but when you're interrupted, get back to work as soon as possible. A business friend of mine has a sign on his desk that says very bluntly: IF YOU HAVE NOTHING TO DO, DON'T DO IT HERE. It really cuts down the congestion in his office.

Upgrade your own performance. Most people tend to look at their own work as routine and get into a rut. They get bored, slough off, and settle for a sub-standard performance. To upgrade the quality of your own work, be a perfectionist —*not a nit-picker*—for 30 days. Take pains with each detail of your own work.

One of your most important jobs as a manager is to make yourself understood in all your communication. No matter what your specific job as a manager is, chances are you'll find yourself spending most of your time writing more and more letters, memorandums, inter-office correspondence, and reports.

For the next 30 days, be a perfectionist in your writing. Do your letters over as many times as you have to until they say *exactly* what you mean. Simplify the words; shorten the sentences. One of the secrets of good writing is to use the simplest words and the shortest sentences possible that will still clearly express your meaning.

If you're having trouble saying what you really mean in your writing, if you're writing another letter or memorandum to explain what you said in the first one, if you're getting telephone calls asking you to clarify your letters, if you read your own letter the next day and don't understand what you wrote, then get a copy of my book, *How to Put Yourself Across with People,** and read Chapter 4, "How to Make Sure You're Understood."

It will show you how to write with clarity, simplicity, strength, and brevity. You'll learn how to clear the dead-heads out of your writing so you can make your letters clear, strong,

---

* James K. Van Fleet, *How to Put Yourself Across With People* (West Nyack, New York: Parker Publishing Company, 1971).

forceful, and to the point. I unconditionally guarantee that you'll improve your writing and your speaking abilities when you do as it says to do.

Be Enthusiastic

Norman Vincent Peale has spent a lifetime showing people how to be enthusiastic and think positively. His books show people how to get more out of life by using a positive and enthusiastic approach.

Most successful people believe firmly in the need for enthusiasm. Like Bert Putnam, the Assistant Vice-President in Charge of Manufacturing for the Abbott Laboratories, for instance. "Enthusiasm often marks the difference between success and failure," Bert says. "An improper order carried out enthusiastically and with vigor has a much better chance of succeeding than the best order carried out carelessly without spirit or drive."

Here are just a few of the ways you can be enthusiastic and set the example for others to follow:

Give yourself your own pep talk. Who motivates the motivator? You do! The motivator of others must be self-motivating. He must inspire himself and be his own self-starter. If you need your boss to come along and give you a pep talk to fill you with enthusiasm, spirit, and drive, I doubt seriously if you should be a manager. Managers must motivate themselves. So give yourself your own pep talk.

Associate with enthusiastic people. Mix with those who are excited about their work and interested in the future. Some of their enthusiasm is bound to rub off on you. If you can't do that too well in your work, then do it when you're off the job by associating with enthusiastic people, or . . .

Read some positive thinking books to fire up your enthusiasm. It's hard today to think positive when the newspapers are filled with war, crime, pollution, poverty, and so many negative ideas. But you can use part of your day to read some positive, forward thinking, self-help books that show you how to improve and how to get more out of life. If you don't know how or where to start, I'd suggest you get David Dunn's book, *Try Giving Yourself Away,** and try some of his ideas. They helped me; I know they'll help you.

Be enthusiastic about your job.   When my house was being built, my wife and I used to go out every so often to watch the progress. One day I asked one of the bricklayers on the job a question about construction and he said, "I don't know. You'd better ask the boss. I'm only a bricklayer."

"And a marvelous one, too," I replied. "I've been watching you work. You make bricklaying an art; you add the master's touch. I could never do it as well as you do."

He was still beaming and bubbling enthusiastically over his work when I left two hours later.

Think of the people who depend on your example.   Whenever your enthusiasm lags, remember you're the motivator; they're the motivated. Keep that idea foremost in your mind and it'll perk you up like magic when you realize how much your people need you.

Use Your Initiative

Initiative is the *power of commencing.* It is seeing what has to be done and initiating a course of action, even in the absence of orders. As Hannibal said, "I will find a way or make one." Your people will unite quickly behind you when you meet new and unexpected situations and problems with prompt and decisive action.

You can encourage initiative among your people by assigning them work commensurate with their abilities and then allowing them to work out the details and finish the job.

Closely associated with initiative is *resourcefulness,* the ability to deal with a situation or solve a problem in the absence of normal means or methods. Inactivity or passive acceptance of an unsatisfactory situation, because of the lack of normal means or conventional methods of handling it, is never justified.

Today we have transistors in our radios, our television sets, our hi-fi systems and tape recorders to replace the old-fashioned

---

* David Dunn, *Try Giving Yourself Away* (Englewood Cliffs, New Jersey: Prentice-Hall, Inc. 1970).

vacuum tubes. Why? Because someone used his initiative and came up with a better idea.

A transistor is only one tiny example of the technical progress we've made just because someone had a better idea or a better way of doing things. Every invention, from the first crude wheel to the intricate and highly sophisticated control system of a manned space rocket to the moon, came about because of someone's initiative and resourcefulness.

Initiative comes in three parts: *seeing what needs to be done; thinking about possible solutions; taking the action to do the job.* So if you're going to use your initiative to get things done as a manager, those are the three things you'll have to do: *see, think, act.*

"Initiative can be developed," says Martin H. Lewis, head of Monsanto's research and development division. "It can be developed by giving a man a difficult—if not impossible—job to do (like landing a man on the moon) and forcing him to come up with a way to do it. As his abilities increase, make his next task even more difficult, and you'll force him to continually develop his initiative to get the job done."

Here's how you can use your initiative to get the job done and set the example for your people to follow at the same time:

1. Stay mentally and physically alert.
2. Train yourself to recognize tasks that need to be done and then do them without being told to do so.
3. Think up new approaches to problems.
4. Learn to anticipate by thinking ahead.
5. Make the most of promising new ideas or plans.
6. Look for and readily accept responsibility.
7. Put into operation worthwhile suggestions made by your people.
8. Encourage them to try new methods and new ideas.
9. Utilize all your available resources in the most effective and efficient manner possible.

It may have come as a surprise to you to discover that in this chapter I have not discussed such personal qualities as bearing, dress, language, morals, and the sort of thing we normally call "Sunday School virtues," to set the example for others to follow. Don't misunderstand me, please. It's not that I have anything against these fine qualities; I haven't. Nor is it that I feel they're not important; I do.

However, I do feel you've progressed far beyond the stage where I should be telling you what to do or not to do in your own personal behavior, or preaching a sermon.

First of all, I'm not qualified to do that. Second, I feel this way: I'm the only person in the world whose morals I really have to worry about.

THIRTEEN

Trying to Be Liked Rather Than Respected

We all want to be liked. It's a natural desire. Managers are certainly no exception. But if you try to make a career out of just being liked, you're making a big mistake. It's far more important that you be respected by your people. Then chances are they'll like you, too.

George S. was promoted to the position of supervisor from the labor force in a large furniture manufacturing plant. He was retained in the same department so the company could use his technical skills and experience to the maximum.

George wanted to succeed in his new job, but he was also anxious to keep his friendships intact with his former co-workers so they wouldn't think he was putting on airs and trying to lord it over them.

"What I do in the plant on company time is the company's business," he told himself. "What I do on my own time is my own business. The only thing that really matters is what I do on the job."

George continued to go to a local tavern for a few beers with his men when they got off work. He rolled the dice and played horses with them for drinks just as before. Sometimes a few beers became too many, and when a man drank too much, George gave him the morning off, knowing he'd be useless at work with a hangover, anyway.

So the word went out that nothing had changed. "No sweat," the men told each other. "George is the same old George. Promotion to supervisor hasn't changed him one bit."

And George did find it hard to reprimand a man or discipline him at work when he'd been out partying with him the night before.

He overlooked their mistakes more and more. He let them get by with prolonging their coffee breaks and lunch periods. Nor did he say anything when people were late to work. He accepted all sorts of ridiculous excuses for absenteeism. He even approved work that he himself would have been ashamed of doing a few short weeks before.

In less than two months after George had taken over the department, it was in a complete shambles. Production had fallen off . . . quality had slipped badly . . . accidents had increased . . . several hundred yards of expensive fabric had been ruined . . . housekeeping had become sloppy and slipshod . . . the men were careless about everything.

Then the plant manager called for George. "I've been waiting for you to get on your feet and get things under control," he said. "I realized you were new on the job so I wanted to give you every opportunity to get things straightened out, but I can't wait forever. You have 30 days to get your department back in shape. If you don't, you're through."

Naturally, George was scared. He'd tried to be a good fellow to get the job done and he'd failed. So he figured he'd have to be an SOB to succeed. He tried to regain control by tightening the screws and getting tough with his men, but it was too late. They rebelled completely. There was flagrant disobedience of orders; machinery broke down for lack of oil and water; maintenance and repair men found wrenches and screwdrivers jammed into wheels and gear boxes.

So management gave up and fired George. They figured the only way to get the department back under control was to start all over again with a brand-new supervisor—a complete stranger—and that they did.

George made the mistake of trying to assume the responsibilities of a new position that made him the boss over his former co-workers and trying to retain the same old friendly relationships with them at the same time. The result was total failure. It didn't work for George and it won't work for you. It never does.

Admittedly the company made a mistake, too. They would have been far better off not to keep George in the same department when they promoted him, even though they wanted to utilize his special technical skills and abilities in that department, but that isn't the real reason for his failure. George is still primarily at fault, for *he placed more emphasis on being liked than on being respected.* Therefore he could only *demand* respect. Had he placed more emphasis on being respected rather than on being liked, he'd have been able to *command* respect insteading of demanding it.

When you're not wasting your time and spinning your wheels as George did trying to be liked rather than respected . . .

YOU'LL GAIN THESE BENEFITS

1. You won't have to put on a false front; you can be yourself.
2. You won't have to use soft soap and flattery and butter up your employees to get the job done.
3. You won't have to win any popularity contest. In fact, you won't even have to enter one.
4. You can just act normal. You won't have to participate in those silly games people play trying to impress others.
5. Your subordinates will do much better work for you.
6. They'll willingly carry out your wishes and your desires.
7. You'll gain their loyalty, cooperation, and support.
8. What's more—they'll even like you.

To show you how to gain these benefits, I've divided the methods you can use into two main parts: *Do's* and *Don'ts.* First, the *Don'ts:*

NEGATIVE TECHNIQUES YOU CAN USE

Don't Accept Favors from Your Subordinates

This is a standing rule—even though sometimes violated —in the armed services, government, and in most companies and corporations. The point is, the moment you accept a favor from someone, you're obligating yourself to do one for him in return. At any level, this can lead to inefficiency, blackmail, bribery, and corruption.

Some people try to evade this rule by giving presents to the boss's wife. Don't accept one for your wife and don't let her accept one either.

Not only should you not accept presents or gifts from your subordinates, but you should also avoid accepting any favors at all that could force you into a compromising position.

For instance, one of the biggest mistakes you can make along this line would be to ask a subordinate to cover for you when you're late or absent.

"I made that mistake when I was a young department supervisor," says Dale Alexander, Vice-President in charge of manufacturing for Organic Food Products, Inc., a health food manufacturing firm in Long Beach, California. "My wife was pregnant and having a lot of trouble. I was on the graveyard shift—11 PM to 7 AM—and I'd slip away for a couple of hours each night to be with her. I asked one employee—a man I thought I could trust—to call me if I was needed, but not to let anyone know I was gone.

"At the end of a month, I knew I'd made a bad mistake, for he began asking for all sorts of favors in return: raise in pay, promotion, even wanted me to punch the clock for him when he was late. When I told him I couldn't do these things, he reminded me of my nightly absences.

"I was in a corner and I realized I'd been a fool. I went to my boss and told him the truth. I expected to get the axe. But he didn't fire me, simply because I'd finally got up the courage to go to him.

"'You've learned your lesson,' he said. 'Now you know you can't accept favors from your subordinates. I don't want to lose you now. You'll be a much better man to the company as a result of your mistake.'"

It's also wise to apply this same rule to your relationship with people who supply your company if you're in that kind of management position.

"There's nothing wrong with your having friends in companies with whom you do business," says Lawrence Scott, Chief of the Purchasing Department of Consolidated Industries, Inc., in Denver, Colorado. "However, this friendship cannot include the giving or receiving of gifts.

"If a supplier gives me a gift, he's implying that he has to con me into buying his product because I'm not really honest.

I'm cheating on my company by selling out to the bidder who'll give me something instead of doing business with the most qualified one. Gifts lead to kickbacks, and before long you're in over your head and you can't get out. The best way to get out is to stay out and not get in."

Don't Do Special Favors Trying to Be Liked

This is not to imply that you shouldn't try to help your employees whenever, however, and wherever you can. You should help them, of course, on the job, and with their personal problems if they ask for help in solving them. But it does mean you shouldn't overlook a man's faults on the job, his bad work, tardiness, absenteeism, and the like, as a special favor to him so he'll like you. This is what led to George's downfall, and it can lead to yours, too.

Don't Try to Make Popular Decisions

Popularity is short lived. Singers and musical groups come and go, dependent upon the moods, the whims, and the fancies of their audiences. Just remember that *your job is to be a manager—not to win some popularity contest.*

If you want to last as a manager, don't go for short-term popularity by trying to make decisions that people like. You place yourself completely at the mercy of your employees when you do this. You owe it to yourself, your company, and your subordinates to make the right decision. This isn't always the popular thing to do, perhaps, but it's the best. Your decisions will last longer and so will you.

Don't Be Soft About Enforcing Discipline

If a man knows the punishment for a certain act but he does it anyway, don't let him off the hook just because you feel sorry for him, or because he promises not to do it again. If you don't stick to your principles, he'll do it again, and yet again, and that's for sure.

Punish with compassion and justice, but punish. If you feel the specified punishment is too severe, you must do everything you can to get it changed and modified. But as long as it's in effect, you must do your best to enforce it.

Judge Harlan Stevens, a prominent west coast jurist, says it this way: "If the law is wrong, then you must take active steps to get the law changed. But until that happens—until it's off the books—you have no choice but to obey it, and I have no choice but to enforce it. If every judge in the country were to start making his own laws, our society would soon fall completely apart."

Don't Party or Socialize with Your Employees

I have nothing against good fellowship and I enjoy getting together with people for a social function as much as anyone else, but I've never done it with my subordinates. And I've yet to meet the executive or manager who's been able to do that successfully.

I don't say this because I'm some sort of social snob. I'm no better than anyone else. My reason is both practical and logical. You see, when you've entertained a man in your home or when you've rubbed elbows with him at a bar, it's extremely hard to reprimand or criticize him the next morning or to fire him if that drastic action becomes necessary.

Sure it's nice to be well liked by the people who work for you, but social relationships with your employees will interfere with your company responsibilities, distort your good sense of judgment, and cause you to fail as a manager.

Just remember that *when the boss gets involved socially with his subordinates, he's no longer the boss!*

Don't Place Yourself in a Compromising Position with Your Employees

If you follow the previous *Don'ts*, chances are you won't find yourself in this pickle. This problem comes up when a manager decides to take money under the table, accepts a gift from a subordinate or a supplier, gets involved with a female employee, or any number of things along this line. You leave yourself wide open for at least petty blackmail, perhaps even worse.

POSITIVE TECHNIQUES YOU CAN USE

You can use a variety of positive methods to gain the respect of your subordinates. To tell the truth, if you practice the techniques I've shown you in all the other chapters of this book, your people will respect you.

I was hard put to write the rest of this chapter, not because of a scarcity of material, but because of an overabundance. Finally, I decided to tell you about a man I knew a long time ago—a gentleman I respected more than any other I've ever known.

His name was Charles T. McCampbell. He was a Major in the United States Army back in the thirties, before World War II, when being a West Point graduate and a regular army officer really meant something. Not that it doesn't mean something now, but in those days the army was much smaller and the standards were so high that few people made it.

Major McCampbell knew his job and he knew it well. He conducted himself as a gentleman at all times. I never once saw him lose his temper. This is not to say he never felt anger, but that he always kept his emotions under tight control, no matter how trying the circumstances.

Although he was intensely loyal to his superiors, he had no fear of them. He also stuck up for his own people and was just as loyal to them, too. He was frank and honest, and said what he meant and meant what he said. In all the years I knew him he never lied, nor did he ever once fail to keep his word. He never abused his privileges as an officer, as some were often prone to do.

The Major had a sense of humor and didn't make the mistake of taking himself too seriously. He was kind, decent, courteous, and he respected fully the rights of others. Although he felt responsible for setting the example for his subordinates to follow, he didn't place himself up on a pedestal or become a bore by preaching, sermonizing, or moralizing. He never tried to set up his own standards of right and wrong.

All in all, he was a man's man and such a man comes along but seldom. He died in France in World War II, more than 25 years ago, but I thought of him again just the other day when my wife gave me a birthday card that read, "Just had to wish happy birthday to someone who is wonderful, kind, considerate, cheerful, delightful, and easy to get along with . . . after all, there are so few of our kind left any more."

I doubt if the message on the card fitted me (except from my wife's point of view, perhaps, but after all, she is prejudiced!), but it did seem like an appropriate description of him.

Let's go over just a few of the Major's positive points now, so you can learn how to gain respect from your people just as he did from his.

Know Your Job

As a manager, you must be able to plan and organize the work. You must order and direct, and then supervise to make sure it gets done. When you know your job, your people will have confidence in you and respect you. Job knowledge is a fundamental of managership.

I know of no finer compliment you can receive than to overhear one of your employees say, "Go ask the old man about it; he'll know exactly what to do."

Conduct Yourself As a Gentleman at All Times

You could tick off a long list of things here that you ought to do if you want to be regarded as a gentleman. I'd like to simplify that procedure for you like this: *When you treat every man as a gentleman and every woman as a lady, you can't help but be a gentleman yourself.* You just couldn't be otherwise.

Have a Sense of Humor

This is not to say that you have to be a comedian, make yourself the butt of every joke, or make fun of yourself as Jack Benny and Red Skelton always used to do. But if you do have a sense of humor, you can learn to roll with the punch and not make a federal case out of every little problem.

When you have a sense of humor, you'll not be inclined to put yourself up on that pedestal. People who put themselves above others tend to be overly serious, conceited, disgustingly self-important and self-righteous. Be an example to be followed —not a model to be admired.

Be Loyal to Both Your Superiors and Your Subordinates

You must be loyal to those above you. If you are not, you cannot be an effective member of the team; nor can you earn the respect, trust, and confidence of your superiors.

If you are a carping critic of your superiors, if you constantly question their orders, their directives, their intelligence —especially in front of your subordinates—you become a drag on the organization.

It is impossible to gain the respect of your subordinates by criticizing your superiors. If you can't be loyal to the man who pays your salary, then you really ought to go to work for someone else.

Loyalty is a two-way street. One of the best ways you can earn the loyalty of your subordinates is to act as a *buffer* between them and your superiors. This doesn't mean that you are to lie or cover up for your employees. It means you are to protect them from unwarranted punishment and undue criticism from above. You can best do that by telling your superior, "His mistake is my responsibility; I'll see that it's taken care of."

You can show your loyalty to those who work for you by giving each man the opportunity for advancement when he has earned it. You should reward superior achievement. You can't win respect from them if you play favorites and reward the undeserving.

Use the Golden Rule Attitude

If you do good to another, you will do good to yourself. Do evil to another and you will do evil to yourself. The Golden Rule, *do unto others as you would have others do unto you,* can be changed around a bit to read *what you do to others— they will likewise do to you.* Let's see how that works out in practical everyday usage.

- Be kind to others—they will be kind to you.
- Be mean to others—they will be mean to you.
- Be courteous to others—they will be courteous to you.
- Be rude to others—they will be rude to you.
- Be friendly to others—they will be friendly to you.
- Be hostile to others—they will be hostile to you.
- *Have respect for others—they'll have respect for you.*

Since that's the one we're after in this chapter, let's stop right there. No need to go any further.

If you will use the techniques I've given you here, you'll find you can have your cake and eat it, too. That is to say, *you'll be liked and respected all at the same time.*

FOURTEEN

Failing to <u>Give</u> Cooperation to <u>to</u> Your Employees

Most managers complain that they don't *get* enough cooperation from their employees. When I first started to write this section, I was thinking along that same old line, too. In fact, the first title I gave this chapter was "Failing to Get Cooperation from Your Employees." But the words wouldn't come, so after several days of wasted effort, I gave Joe Ewing, the local Sears Roebuck store manager, a call and asked him for advice.

"You're taking the wrong approach, Jim," he said. "You're looking at it the wrong way. Most managers and executives and businessmen say the same thing. They all complain that they don't *get* enough cooperation *from* their employees. But why don't they? What's their real problem? Who's actually at fault—the managers or their employees?

"I can tell you right now the managers are at fault, Jim. And what's more, I can also tell you where they're making their basic mistake. I know, because I made that same mistake myself for many years before I realized what I was doing wrong.

"They're not *giving* any cooperation *to* their employees first. That's why they're not getting any in return. *You must always give before you can expect to get. When you do, you'll always get back more than you give away.* Think of cooperation that way, Jim, and you won't have any trouble at all."

And I realized that Joe was right. Once my thinking got straightened out, the ideas came like rain and the words began to flow again.

When you, too, cooperate with your employees first—

135

YOU'LL GAIN THESE BENEFITS

1. Your employees will cooperate with you.
2. Even your problem employees will cooperate, too.
3. They'll respect you and have confidence in you.
4. You'll gain their willing obedience, their unswerving loyalty, and their wholehearted support.
5. They'll work with initiative, ingenuity, and enthusiasm.
6. They'll work together as a team with high spirit and morale, with a definite purpose and direction toward a common goal.
7. You'll make them feel they belong where they are.
8. They'll work just as hard as you do to get the job done.

TECHNIQUES YOU CAN USE TO GAIN THESE BENEFITS

Let me say right off I could give you a lot of routine orthodox ways of doing things to show you how to gain cooperation from your employees by cooperating with them first. For instance, I could say you ought to do your part in establishing good human relationships by giving a man fair pay with salary increases . . . job security . . . interesting and worthwhile work to do . . . opportunity for advancement . . . promotion by a merit system. I will say all these are important; you must give an employee these things, too. But I assume you're doing most of them already.

So in this section I'm going to cover points the average manager doesn't pay much attention to—perhaps has never even thought about. That's why he's average. You can be far above average by including them in your repertoire of management skills. Use these techniques and you'll add much to your professional stature as a manager.

You Must Give of Yourself First

If you want cooperation and teamwork from your employees, then you must *give them your cooperation and teamwork first*. Top managers know this secret. They've mastered the art of getting their employees to cooperate with them by giving them their cooperation first.

You can easily tell if you're giving cooperation to your employees, too. If they're prompt and cheerful, filled with enthusiasm, enjoy their work and are ready to put in an extra lick or so when it's necessary, or when you ask them to—you can be sure you're doing the right thing as a manager or section supervisor.

But if you're not giving your employees your cooperation, you can tell that easily enough, too. They'll be just as uninterested in cooperating with you as you are with them. They'll drag into work late, do a mediocre job all day, and run for the time clock even before the whistle blows. If that's the way your employees act in your department, don't make the mistake of asking them for anything extra. You'll not get it.

Please keep this in mind, not only as you read the rest of this chapter, but also in your daily relationships with other people—your associates, superiors, customers—as well as your employees.

You must always give if you want to get, and you get back exactly what you give away, although the return is usually multiplied several times over. That's the one sure way of gaining cooperation from your employees as a manager.

Give Him a Second Home in Your Organization

A man spends 30 to 40 years of his life—eight hours a day, five to six days a week—earning a living. Many times, he spends nearly as many hours on his job as he does at home. This being so, one of the wisest things you can do as a manager is give him a second home in your department or section.

"Japanese managers in business and industry could sure teach us a lot about how to cooperate with our employees if we were just willing to learn from them," says Howard L. King, an executive with Coca Cola's export and foreign trade division. "They really know how to use practical, everyday applied psychology with their people. I spent many years in Japan for my company and I was always impressed by the way Japanese companies take care of their workers.

"For instance, they offer a tremendous number of fringe benefits—like completely furnished dormitories that are neat and clean and extremely livable—separate cottages if they're married—cafeteria and recreation facilities including movies, tennis courts, golf courses, and bowling alleys, a discount store, a company credit union—and in fact, everything possible to make an employee feel he's really a member of their family, not just another time-clock-number on the payroll. Most of these fringe benefits are furnished completely free, too. The benefits the workers do pay for are given to them at cost.

"The Japanese way of doing things is to *give* everything possible to the worker to *get* the best possible cooperation from him. Don't make the mistake of comparing their system with the company store that used to exist, and still does in some places in America, for the miner and the migrant farm worker. In the United States, the company tried to bind the worker to the organization by keeping him in debt to them and to make an exorbitant profit at the same time. That is definitely not the Japanese concept. If it were, it wouldn't work, any more than it does in America. Japanese business and industry couldn't possibly gain the loyal cooperation of their employees the way they do."

I've seen the Japanese system at close range myself, and I can vouch for what Mr. King says. For example, the loyalty of a Japanese worker to his company or his employer is almost as strong as his parental ties. If he causes his firm to lose face, he takes it just as seriously as if he had disgraced his own family. He always refers to the company as "my" company, and the word *my* is written with the same Japanese character that means *family*.

In Japan, cooperation begins at the top—not at the bottom. Japanese firms take care of their employees almost from the cradle to the grave. If a male worker marries a girl employed by the same firm, there is cause for great rejoicing on management's part. They feel the bond of loyalty to the company has been strengthened even more by having a husband-and-wife team—not just a man and woman—working for them.

Does their system work? Well, as I say, I've been in Japan, too, and I've visited some of their factories in the Tokyo and Yokohama areas. I've seen Japanese workers cheer each other when they were changing shifts, like baseball players applauding a teammate who's just hit a home run. Have you ever seen that in your department? And I've seen entire office staffs assembled at Tokyo International Airport to wish their boss good luck and see him off on an important business trip. Anyone ever do that for you? I've also seen them start the day off in the plant by singing the company song. Is that the way the employees in your section start off their work day?

If you still have doubts about how successful their methods are, look around you at the numerous fine quality products they make, like Sony tape recorders, Panasonic stereo sets, Canon and Nikkon cameras, Toyota and Datsun automobiles, Honda and Suzuki motorcycles. Or take a look at Japan's position in world economics as one of the world's biggest exporters of top lines of merchandise. She's right up there with a lot of quality products.

I know you'll be limited in what you can do as a department manager or a section supervisor to *give* cooperation *to* your employees. But if you'll do some digging, you can come up with a lot of simple ways to provide small rewards within your department or section to recognize the efforts and the achievements of your workers.

Perhaps you can give a conscientious worker a little time off when he needs it for some personal business. Maybe you can even "bend the rules" just a bit to help a deserving long-time employee. Or if a person makes a suggestion for changing procedures, you can collaborate by trying his idea, even though you might have doubts whether it will work or not. At least show your willingness to cooperate by trying his methods.

Sometimes it can be as simple as sending out for coffee and doughnuts for people who are working late. A small gesture on your part can mean much to hard-working faithful employees. If you can't think of any specific methods to use, here are . . .

FOUR TECHNIQUES YOU CAN USE AS A DEPARTMENT MANAGER OR SECTION SUPERVISOR TO GIVE COOPERATION TO YOUR EMPLOYEES

Give Him a Chance to Participate in Management

As Jimmy Durante always used to say, "Everybody wants to get into the act." Your employees want to have a say in how things are run. You can make them feel it's *their* department, too, by letting them have a part in the planning, decision making, formulation of rules and regulations, policies and procedures. You can use any number of ways to let your employees participate in management so you can gain their cooperation.

Give Them the Opportunity to Help Make the Rules

One of the problems encountered in the traditional way rules are formulated and administered is that managers at the top of the organization dictate what is right and wrong for workers at the bottom.

Top management in the average company arbitrarily sets the rules for employees to follow. So do department managers and section supervisors. But most people don't like being told what to do or what not to do. After all, rules are restrictions on their personal liberties. So they tend to resist the rules or disobey them.

One of the best ways you can cooperate with your employees in your department is to let them work out the rules and regulations to follow and submit them to you for approval. You'll find the average employee will be much stricter on himself than you are. And since these rules are *his* rules, the ones *he* made up, he'll be much more likely to follow them than if they were yours alone.

Give Your Emloyees a Chance to Take Part in Decisions

When the people in your department feel they've had a say in the decision-making process, they're much more likely to cooperate with you. If they agree with the decision they'll look at it as if it were their very own and they'll back it to the hilt. If they don't agree, they'll still back it more strongly than they would otherwise, simply because you gave them the courtesy of considering their point of view fully and fairly.

Hold Weekly Conferences

People like to know what's going on. They like to be let in on things so they can see how their efforts in your department relate to overall company goals and achievements. You might call your employees together on Monday morning, for instance, for a short 15-minute meeting to discuss what's needed for the coming week.

This would be a good time to encourage reports on problems or work difficulties in your section and to talk about new developments for the future. It would also be an appropriate time to pass out compliments. You can also encourage your people to voice their complaints and let them work the steam out of their systems. You can cooperate by first listening and then taking the necessary corrective action if the problem can be resolved at your level, or by reporting it to your boss if you can't handle it.

SUGGESTIONS YOU CAN MAKE TO YOUR BOSS AS A DEPARTMENT MANAGER OR SECTION SUPERVISOR TO ENCOURAGE EMPLOYEE COOPERATION

When you're a department manager or a section supervisor, you don't have the final say. I know that from experience. But at least you can make suggestions. If your boss accepts them, fine. If he doesn't, no harm done.

For instance, just to get your thinking off in the right direction, you might consider offering such suggestions as company-sponsored softball teams or bowling leagues; company-owned and maintained tennis and volleyball courts; a gymnasium where employees can work out; an indoor swimming pool; a recreation hall with ping-pong tables and billiard tables; a picnic grounds or camping area for the outdoor types; a credit union; a discount store or buying service.

If you feel that none of these are appropriate to discuss with your boss, then use your initiative and come up with some of your own. After all, you know your boss far better than I do.

I do know of three specific companies who use three concrete methods to gain better employee cooperation. Perhaps your boss would be more interested in them since they're already proven winners. Here's what they are:

Suggest an Employee Stock Purchase Plan at a Reduced Cost to Your Boss

"One of the best ways I've ever found to get my employees to cooperate in getting the job done is to get them to buy some stock in the company," says Wayne Walker, President and Chief Executive Officer of Walker Plastics Incorporated in Tulsa, Oklahoma. "The moment he becomes a stockholder, his attitude changes. So we offer our people the privilege of purchasing stock in the company at a reduced cost. When a man becomes a stockholder in the company he works for, he has a real reason to cooperate and produce."

Sears Roebuck has always been a leader in using an employee stock-purchase plan. It gives their people a definite incentive to cooperate with management, for every employee who owns stock in the company is a quasi-manager himself. Does it work? Well, Sears Roebuck is the biggest retailer in all the world. It must work.

Suggest a Profit-Sharing Plan to Your Boss

Not only can you suggest a special employee stock-purchase plan to your boss to promote and stimulate employee cooperation, but you might also be able to interest him in an employee profit-sharing plan.

A profit-sharing plan is not the same as a wage-incentive plan. Under a wage-incentive plan, the more a man produces, the more he earns *as an individual*. Under a profit-sharing plan, a man shares in the *actual profits* of the entire company. The more the company makes, the more *all* the employees make, so all the workers are anxious to cooperate. Those who do not soon leave.

One of the pioneers of profit-sharing has been the Lincoln Electric Company of Cleveland, Ohio. Mr. James F. Lincoln started it all when he was president. He worked out a plan with his employees so all the workers could share in the profits.

Did profit sharing work for them? You can judge for yourself. Here are some of the results they obtained in the first ten years they used the plan.

1. Annual volume of business increased six and one-half times.
2. Production costs were cut in half despite rising costs.
3. Stockholders' dividends quadrupled.
4. Average employee's wages went up over 400 percent.
5. Employee turn-over was reduced to nearly zero.
6. There were neither strikes nor work slow-downs.

Suggest to Your Boss That He Form a Junior Board of Directors

An excellent way to promote cooperation is to form a junior board of executives from the employee ranks and give them an active part in management. Does that sound too far-fetched or ridiculous to you to suggest to your boss?

Don't laugh. That procedure kept Baltimore's famous old spice and extract firm, McCormick and Company, from going completely broke back in the 1930's.

Charles P. McCormick took over the company when his uncle, Willoughby McCormick—founder of the firm—died in 1932. He initiated a number of new ideas to get the financially sick firm back on its feet. The most successful idea he had was *multiple management.* This was a system he designed to insure maximum worker cooperation and participation, and at the same time, to provide the company with a source of young ambitious managerial talent.

Mr. McCormick appointed what he called a "junior board of directors." That first board had 17 people and was made up of clerks, accountants, assistant department supervisors, and production employees. Their job was to find ways to improve whatever they thought needed improving. They were told to write their own rules and regulations, elect their own officers, and to be self-governing. All the company books and sales records were made available to them.

As a control measure, Mr. McCormick stipulated that all recommendations be unanimous and subject to final approval by the regular board of directors elected by the stockholders.

The plan worked. Within a few years the junior board had redesigned and modernized the company's packaging procedures: there was a sharp rise in sales as a direct result. They worked out better office procedures and cut their overhead and administrative costs; they suggested new products to add to the variety of the line.

Of five thousand suggestions made by that first junior board, over 99 percent were accepted by the senior board of directors. *Mr. McCormick credited the junior board with saving the company from bankruptcy.*

FIFTEEN

Failing to Ask Your Subordinates for Their Advice and Help

"I used to hire efficiency experts and management consultants to the tune of several hundred dollars every time we had a problem we couldn't seem to solve for ourselves," says Walter Morris, President of Penthouse Furniture, Inc., in Asheville, North Carolina. "No more. Let me tell you why I stopped doing that.

"About two years ago we added some new items to our line. We hired over a hundred more employees to handle our increased production. We were already having trouble with our time card and time clock system, and the extra help further increased the long lines and delays in getting people in and out of the plant when we changed shifts.

"It was really a big headache to all of us. We were losing valuable production time. Our employees were complaining about having to come to work early just to be able to punch in on time. When no one in management could come up with any ideas, I called in an efficiency expert as usual to take care of the problem for me.

"He spent about a week in the plant and came up with a solution that worked. I was quite well satisfied, for he'd solved my problem; until one day as I was walking through the plant, one of my oldest employees, Harold Smith, stopped me to ask a question.

"'You know that guy you had in here about a month ago to figure out a new time card and time clock system for you?' he said.

" 'Why, yes—of course I remember, Harold,' I said. 'Why do you ask?'

" 'Well, I was just wondering how much money you wasted,' Harold said. 'You see, I know he must have recommended the method *I told him about* because that's the one you're using now. I'd have told you about it for nothing if you'd just asked me.'

"Harold's remarks got me to thinking, so I checked back through the files and looked at the number of times and the reasons we'd called in outside help to solve our problems for us. Then I asked my employees a lot of questions about their visits, too.

"I found out that most of those so-called efficiency experts and management consultants weren't really so smart after all. Seems that 95 percent of the time the answers they gave me were coming right from my own employees! I could've had those same answers myself if I'd just taken the time to ask for the advice and help of my own people.

"You can bet I don't call in any outsiders any more to solve my business problems. Now I use the money I used to pay them to offer a *reward* to my own employees for coming up with usable ideas and useful suggestions.

"Like right now we've got some problems to be taken care of in our number four production line. I've offered a reward of $300 to the employee who can come up with the right solution. And sooner or later someone will; someone always does."

Maybe you're not the big boss and you can't pay the people in your department cold hard cash for their helpful suggestions, but you can reward them in some way for their ideas. For instance, when it comes time for a promotion, you know your boss will be asking for your recommendation. That's one way you can reward a person. Or see if you can get the authority to give a man a day off with pay as a reward for his idea. Use your own imagination and come up with some suggestions of your own to make to your boss. Could be he'll reward you, too.

At any rate, as you can see, Walter Morris gained some definite benefits for himself when he learned to ask his subordinates for their advice and help. So can you. In fact, here are some of the . . .

BENEFITS YOU'LL GAIN BY ASKING YOUR PEOPLE FOR THEIR ADVICE AND HELP

They'll Feel As Though They're Part of Your Team

When you ask a man for his ideas and his opinions, you're letting him know that he's both needed and wanted by your. No one wants to be a nonentity or just another clock-number on the payroll. Every single person in your organization wants to be part of your team. Everyone wants to feel that he belongs.

When you ask your employees for their advice and help, you give them that individual identity they want so much. You make them members of your team. They'll work much harder for you when they feel they're making a major contribution to the success of your organization.

You Can Identify People of Above Average Ability

One of the best ways to find people of above-average intelligence and ability in your organization is to establish a creative climate and atmosphere. When you ask for specific solutions to definite problems, you automatically set up hurdles and obstacles that test your people's maximum potential. Ask for their advice and help and you'll uncover employees who have above-average ability to help you solve your problems.

You'll Give Your People a Sense of Importance

Although it's important to offer a tangible monetary reward to the person who comes up with a useful and usable item, you'll find that giving him a feeling of importance will be of great benefit to you, too. For example, give him a letter of appreciation or a certificate of achievement along with the financial reward. It will be retained and remembered long after the money's spent and gone.

Your Employees Will Put Their Imagination, Initiative, and Ingenuity to Work for You

Finally, if you're the big boss, you can do as Walter Morris now does. Instead of paying efficiency experts and management consultants several hundred dollars to solve your problems for you, you can pay your employees a reward instead. When you offer a reasonable monetary reward to the person who comes up with a definite solution to a certain stated problem, you are making it quite plain to your people that their ideas are wanted. In fact, you're actively soliciting their help when you offer them a reward. Use that method and your employees will put their imagination, their initiative, and their ingenuity to work for you. They'll use their brains overtime to come up with answers to your problems.

TECHNIQUES YOU CAN USE TO GAIN THE BENEFITS

Get Yourself in the Proper Frame of Mind

The first thing you need to do to be able to ask your employees for their help and advice is to get yourself in the right frame of mind so you'll accept their suggestions when they're offered to you. Don't let your position as manager or your status as an executive get in your way. It can, you know, for after all, you are their superior—they're your subordinates.

"You can't solicit a man's help if you're more concerned about your status than you are with what he has to offer you," says Charles Foster, the founder and owner of Foster Cafeterias, a well-known restaurant chain in Georgia and Florida. "Status can become a real obstacle if you judge the value of a man's ideas by his education, the way he expresses himself, the kind of job he has, the way he dresses, and so on.

"I can think of all sorts of recommendations I failed to accept in the past simply because I didn't take the time to listen to George, the bus boy, or because I thought that Sam couldn't come up with any good ideas since he was only the dishwasher.

"Today I know better. I've learned that all sorts of good ideas for improvement most often come from the man who's actually doing the job. The fact that I happen to be the boss doesn't mean I have a monopoly on brains. I'm willing to listen to anyone who can help me run a better operation, so I can give better service at less cost to my customers."

How can you, too, forget your status and get in a receptive frame of mind yourself? Well, for instance, you can make a small start by doing away with those polite but meaningless "time of day" exchanges with your employees when you tour your place. Stop and really talk to a person for a change. Get him to open up by *asking for his ideas on the operation.*

When you do ask for his advice, his help, or his ideas, you must really mean it—you must be sincere. Don't do it with tongue in cheek. Don't ask for his advice if all you want is reassurance from him that you're right. If you're sincere about wanting help, your people will know. They'll appreciate your trust in them and your confidence in their knowledge and their abilities. And they'll want to help you.

Make Them Feel It's Their Problem, Too

All of us are more interested in our own problems than we are in someone else's problems. For instance, I know you're more interested in your problems than you are in mine. And your employees are more interested in theirs than they are in yours. So if you want to get your employees interested in your problem—*you must make your problem theirs.* Here's how:

When you ask John for his advice and counsel in solving your problem, when you acknowledge your ignorance and ask him to help you or show you how to do it, you challenge his ingenuity. The moment he becomes interested in helping you solve your problem, it automatically becomes his problem as well.

"One of the toughest problems I had to solve when I took over the management of this store was getting my department heads to cut costs," says Harry Simpson, manager of a Baldwin Discount Center in Little Rock, Arkansas. "But that's why I'd been sent here in the first place: to cut costs and overhead and increase net profits. This store was showing the least profit of all the Baldwin Discount Centers and the owners wanted some definite corrective action taken to change that.

"The previous manager told me he'd tried preaching, sermonizing, pleading, appealing to honor, duty, and loyalty, but with absolutely no results. So when I took over I didn't try any of these methods. I didn't preach or scold. I didn't tell people they had to cut costs or else.

"Instead, *I made cutting costs their problem by forming a committee of all department heads in the store to help me.* I told them I wanted their counsel and advice. Rather than issue a lot of useless orders and directives, I asked them to come up with ideas and suggestions on how to reduce our operating costs.

"I didn't give them any specific areas to cut down on. I left that decision up to them. I just told them it was their problem as well as mine to come up with some ideas on how to cut our overhead. I knew from experience that once they made some suggestions *of their own* for improvement, they would support their own ideas.

"They got their heads together and came up with all sorts of suggestions on how to save money on utilities, warehousing and storage, customer delivery service, packaging and shipping, even postage and telephone charges.

"Within six months we had reduced operating costs 28 percent and the store was showing an acceptable profit margin. And all because *I made my problem theirs.* I couldn't have solved it without their support and help."

You can do as Harry Simpson did if you make your problem your employees' problem. Set up your own employee think-tank and give them your headaches to solve. Whatever you do and however you do it, remember that *the fastest way of solving your problem is to make it their problem, too.* Just be sure to reward them when they solve it for you.

If you can't fatten a man's pay check when he helps you solve your problem, then do as Captain Robert James, a U. S. Army basic training company commander, does in Fort Ord, California. "I can't raise a man's pay when he comes up with a good usable idea," says Captain James. "After all, his pay is controlled by Congress. But I can reward him in other ways, and I do. I can give him a letter of commendation or appreciation . . . I can recommend him for promotion next time there's a vacancy . . . I can give him some time off—a three-day pass, for example. The thing is, I give him the best reward I can. He knows that and he appreciates it."

You can do the same, no matter what your job is as a manager, whether you're a department foreman, a section supervisor, or whatever. Give your people *the best reward you can* for their help. They'll appreciate it and they'll keep doing their best for you, too.

Encourage Individual Thinking, Too

You should not only form groups of people to help you solve your problems, but you should also encourage each individual employee to come up with better ways of doing his own specific job.

First of all, if you want your individual employees to come up with some work improvement ideas, you must let them know you'll listen to their suggestions.

Tell them you realize they know more about their own jobs than anyone else does—including you, the boss. Explain to them you also know there's always room for improvement and that you're counting on them to pinpoint those things for you.

It's always best to ask specific questions if you can to isolate definite areas that need improvement. For instance, you could say,

> "How can we cut down the time between order and delivery for our customers, Mary?"

> "What's your own personal opinion on the cause of this quality problem, Frank?"

> "How can we eliminate this safety hazard on your job, Tim?"

Or if you hear any of your employees complaining about some procedure being a waste of time or costing too much, encourage him to think constructively about how he would change it. Ask him to come up with some possible improvements or to show you a better way. Let him know you really do want his suggestions when you ask for them by offering him an appropriate reward if his methods work.

By giving your employees some concrete problems to solve, you'll encourage and stimulate them to do their best thinking for you. You'll give them something to really zero in on with their brains. And that's when a man comes up with his best ideas—when he really has to, when he has something that has to be solved or else. It's hard to get the brain in gear if you don't feed it some material to work with, some problems to solve, some questions to answer.

Make It Easy for Them to Communicate Their Ideas to You

Don't make it hard for a person to submit his ideas to you. Don't get him all tangled up in rules, regulations, office procedures, and red tape by making him put everything down in at least triplicate on some complicated suggestion form your clerk has devised. Remember you're asking an employee for a favor when you ask him to give you his ideas. You can at least do him the favor of making it easy for him to do so.

"There are several methods you can use to make it easy for your employees to submit their ideas directly to you," says Edward Muller, Director of Education and Training Services for United Chemical Corporation. "First of all, design a simple printed *one-page form* that will help the person get all his facts together in one place.

"It should be worded in such a way that he'll be able to answer the *who, what, when, where, why,* and *how* about his idea. If a sketch or a drawing is needed, make the services of your drafting department available to him.

"But don't ask him to drop his ideas in a suggestion box. They're far too impersonal. Most of the time suggestion boxes gather only dust or messages like 'Drop dead,' 'Get lost,' and the like. They're most often used by unimaginative organizations that pay only lip service to the concept of asking their employees for advice and help, and then usually because they're required to do so by some higher management level.

"Instead of a suggestion box, you can establish certain hours during the week when your door is open to employees who want to discuss their ideas for improvement with you. Don't talk over his proposal formally with him from behind your desk. That puts him at a distinct disadvantage.

"Come out from behind your symbol of authority and sit down with him at your conference table or a coffee table where you can meet each other as equals and talk over his idea without having that boss-employee atmosphere and relationship.

"Have some coffee brought in, too. Tell your secretary to make sure you're not disturbed. Do everything you can to make him feel relaxed and comfortable so he can concentrate completely on his idea—not on your office protocol."

You can keep an open door as Mr. Muller says, or you can make individual appointments with people to discuss their ideas. An appointment with the boss makes a man feel important . . . it proves you really are interested . . . it shows you consider his ideas vital to your growth and progress.

I would like to say here that not everyone is as opposed to suggestion boxes as Mr. Muller is. A great many companies have used them quite successfully for many years. If your company does use the suggestion box, perhaps the system could be improved by combining Mr. Muller's methods with those of your company. In fact, you might offer that suggestion yourself. It could lead to something good for you.

Follow Through on His Idea

A man's idea is the most important thing in the world to him. Don't disappoint him by dragging your feet, putting it off, or forgetting it.

Get someone to go to work on his idea at once. Evaluate it. See if it will work. Find out if it's an improvement or not. And let him know what's going on. Keep him informed; don't leave him in the dark.

Tell him if his idea is under serious consideration. If you've run into some unexpected problem with it, let him know about that, too. After all, it is his idea. He might be able to come up with some concrete answers for these new complications. At least, he'll know you're working on his suggestion, and that alone will make him happy.

When you keep him informed of all you're doing, that is proof that you do take new ideas seriously. He'll do his best to come up with more and even better suggestions for you in the future.

Don't Forget the Reward

You like to get proper credit and prompt recognition for what you do. So do your people. If you forget or neglect this part, you might as well forget about asking your subordinates for their suggestions and their ideas. You won't get any.

So be quick to show your appreciation for what he's done for you by presenting him with the appropriate reward: a bonus, a raise, a promotion, a letter of appreciation, a certificate of achievement.

When you reward an employee for his efforts, you'll raise the standards of every single person in your organization. You'll stimulate everyone to try and come up with some useful and usable ideas for organizational improvement.

So ask your subordinates for their advice and help, their

suggestions and ideas. You'll get lots of dividends when you do. You'll be able to reduce operating costs. You can better meet your competition. You can increase profits. You'll find better ways of doing things. Everyone in your organization will be working closer to his maximum potential. And that makes your job exciting, lots more fun, and really worthwhile.

But don't take my word for it. Put it to work, and see the results for yourself.

SIXTEEN

Failing to Develop a Sense of Responsibility in Your Subordinates

"An employee who'll do his best work only when the boss is around just isn't worth having," says Harlan B. Reeves, manager of General Electronics' Omaha plant. "We can't use people like that. Why, just look at the size of this place. We have three shifts and more than three thousand employees turning out television sets, radios, and electronic components of all kinds 24 hours a day. I can't live here around the clock, so unless our employees have a feeling of deep responsibility to the company to do their best, we couldn't manage to turn out the fine quality products that we do.

"I've tried a lot of methods throughout the years to develop a strong sense of responsibility in employees. The one I personally have found to be the most effective is to give the person the authority to make his own decisions. I'll go even further than that. I'll say that you never will be able to develop a complete sense of responsibility in a person until you force him to make his own decisions.

"Unless you do that, you'll find yourself doing the job your foremen ought to be doing. They'll be making the decisions that belong to their own supervisors. And the supervisors will actually be doing work on the assembly line that you're paying capable and qualified production employees to do.

"I'm not saying that you can abdicate your own responsibility, but a one-man show is evidence of poor management. A good manager will patiently and carefully instruct his subordinates to make sure they know what is expected of them. He can have them present their plans for doing the work to him for approval, but once approved, he will insist that they get their jobs done without minute guidance and detailed supervision.

"When you give your employees full responsibility to do their own work—when you give them the authority to make their own decisions—when you underwrite their mistakes—you'll encourage and motivate them to exercise initiative and to accept the full responsibility of doing the job properly. You'll help them to develop into more effective individuals and more reliable employees. In the end, you'll have a much more efficient organization than if you were to keep the responsibility and authority all to yourself."

**BENEFITS YOU'LL GAIN
BY DEVELOPING A SENSE OF RESPONSIBILITY IN
YOUR SUBORDINATES**

You'll Develop Mutual Confidence and Respect Between Yourself and Your Subordinates

When you show your subordinates that you trust them to do the job by giving them the authority to make their own decisions, they'll respond by giving you everything they've got. Develop a man's sense of responsibility and you'll increase his confidence in his own abilities to get the job done for you. He'll be proud of himself and of what he does for you; he'll respect you as a boss.

You Can Cut Your Supervision to the Bare Minimum

Although you can never do away completely with the necessity of supervising a man's work, you can reduce that requirement to a bare minimum. Whenever you show confidence in an employee's ability to do his job, when he knows that you trust him to make his own decisions, he'll require far less supervision in his work. He'll be motivated to do a good job whether you're around or not. Develop a strong sense of responsibility in your subordinates and you'll find you have more time for other important aspects of your management position.

Your Subordinates Will Put Their Initiative to Work for You

When you offer a man the chance to assume more responsibility by letting him make his own decisions, he'll want to show you that your trust in him is well placed. He'll put his initiative and resourcefulness, his imagination and ingenuity, to work for you. His desire to assume the responsibility for his own work will contribute markedly to the team efforts of your whole organization.

You'll Always Have a Pool of Trained Man-Power Available

Develop a strong sense of responsibility in each subordinate to do not only his own individual job, but *his superior's job* as well. Then you'll always have trained personnel ready for promotion. This technique has been used successfully by Sears Roebuck and J. C. Penney for many years. Use it yourself and you'll find you won't have to waste your time and money training and re-training men hired from the outside.

TECHNIQUES YOU CAN USE TO GAIN THESE BENEFITS

Allow Him Freedom of Expression

If you want your employee to develop a complete sense of responsibility for his own work, then you should let him work in his own style as much as possible. If your people are competent and capable of doing the job, if you trust them enough to do their work properly, then it won't hurt to loosen the reins of authority and let them do things their own way once in a while.

Every employee who works for you should have the right to make his own job more interesting by doing it his way, just as long as it doesn't interfere with the overall efficiency of your operation. All you need do is make sure you're getting the results you want and that your employee isn't violating any safety rule or *reasonabl*e company policy.

"No matter how routine the job might be, a person is going to find some way to insert his own individuality into his work," says Herb Wallace, department foreman at the Felton Steel Casting Company's plant in Milwaukee, Wisconsin. "This expression of his can be either positive or negative. It'll all depend on how you handle him.

"If you want his expression of individuality to become a positive motivating force that will work to your benefit, then you must give him the right to make his job his very own by doing it his own way as much as humanly possible. If you don't do that, your employee will express himself in a negative way on his job that can hurt your or your company.

"For instance, over on that cutting machine, one of our employees placed a small rubber mat under her feet to ease the strain on her legs. Nothing wrong with that; no safety hazard involved. But her supervisor removed it because it spoiled the *uniform appearance* in his section.

"Immediately her production fell off, both in quantity and quality, even though she works on an incentive basis. Soon that whole section was falling behind in output. She was expressing herself in the only way left available to her and her fellow workers were supporting her.

"Now everything's running smoothly again. After a little help from me, her supervisor got the point. He bought her a new rubber mat out of his own pocket and apologized to her for his arbitrary actions. Her production is now even higher than it used to be because she's been allowed to express herself in a very small way on her job."

Experiments in industry have shown that people work more efficiently, even on assembly-line operations, when they're allowed some freedom of individual expression, no matter how small. For example, employees who are given some leeway as to what time to take their coffee breaks are more contented with their work and more motivated to do a good job than when arbitrary coffee break times are set by management.

A salesman who's allowed to schedule his own road trips is more likely to work harder, see more customers in less time, and get more done than if he were forced to follow an itinerary published by the front office.

So do what you can to allow your own people freedom of expression in their own jobs. You can start by looking around your shop to find out how many employees are standing up to do a job when they could do it just as well sitting down. Chances are they'll do an even better job for you sitting down, for it takes more energy to stand than to sit. And the energy they save by sitting down can be expended much more profitably on production for you.

Use Mission-Type Orders As Much As Possible

If you'll remember, we discussed mission-type orders back in Chapter Seven. At that time I told you that mission-type orders would keep you from meddling in details or the work that belongs to someone else.

Here I want to let you know that using mission-type orders is one of the best possible ways to develop a sense of responsibility in your subordinate. They will also allow him that freedom of expression we discussed just a moment ago and let him use his imagination, initiative, and ingenuity to get the job done for you.

So tell your subordinate supervisors what you want them to do, but don't tell them how to do it. Leave the how-to up to them. Hold them completely responsible for getting the results you want, but not for the methods they use to get those results. Delegate the responsibility and supervise their work, but don't interfere unless it's absolutely necessary.

About the only time you'll need to interfere is when an overly zealous subordinate risks the health or safety of his people in getting the job done. If that happens, you'll have to step in, exert your authority as a manager, and take over. As soon as things are back under control again and your subordinate understands his mistake, give him back the responsibility again. If he can't handle it after that, could be you need to let him go permanently.

Give Each Man the Responsibility to Learn His Superior's Job

A good way to develop a sense of responsibility in an employee is to have him learn the detailed duties of his superior's job, and let him do that job as often as possible. You'll gain a couple of big benefits when you do.

First of all, you'll soon develop a pool of trained man-power who can handle the jobs of their superiors if they're sick, on vacation, and the like. You'll also make a man realize that he does have a definite opportunity for promotion and you'll motivate him to do even better on his own job for you.

Many top-notch companies have used this technique of having each employee learn his superior's job successfully for many years. Two companies especially well-noted for this are Sears Roebuck and J. C. Penney.

For example, Sears Roebuck never hires their store managers *off the street*. They work their way up through the company. The retirement of one senior supervisor at Sears can mean the promotion of no less than 14 other persons.

Even the top executive at Sears has to start at the bottom. For instance, Austin T. Cushman became chairman of the board in 1962, 30 years after he joined them in Oakland, California, as a *part-time salesman*.

It's also a standard policy in the J. C. Penney company that everyone must start at the bottom. In fact, every top Penney executive has done so. They have developed this idea of having their people accept responsibility so much that at Penney's they are not called employees; they are called *associates*.

I once asked a top Penney associate how they would replace the chairman of the board if something happened to him, and he said with a straight face, "We'd just hire a new office clerk." And I believe him.

You can put these ideas to work in your own company. Have every person know the duties and details of his superior's job, and then let him do that job every chance he gets. There's no better way for him to learn it.

If you don't give your people this chance to work in the next higher position just because you're afraid something might go wrong or because it's too much trouble, you'll never know what their real potential is. Nor will you ever know who's the most qualified person for promotion. So do it. Who knows? You might become as big as Sears Roebuck or J. C. Penney yourself one of these days.

When You Give Him Responsibility, Give Him Authority, Too

You can't delegate the responsibility for getting the job done if you won't at the same time give the person the authority to carry out his responsibilities. Whenever you give a person the responsibility to do a specific job, you must also give him the authority to do it. *Authority and responsibility go hand in hand.* You cannot separate them.

"The delegation of authority commensurate with the responsibility develops a mutual confidence and respect between you and your subordinates," says Ralph Neale, Operations Manager for the Burlington Northern in Chicago. "It also encourages your subordinates to exercise their initiative to get the job done, and at the same time, to give you their whole-hearted cooperation."

Use the J. C. Penney method.   The J. C. Penney Company is well noted for giving a man the authority to carry out his responsibilities. In their system the store manager is the key man. He is held completely responsible for the management and operation of his own store. At the same time, he is also given full authority to run that store.

He hires and trains his own help: his salesmen and clerks. He makes the decisions about his own local advertising. He orders most of his stock from lists and samples sent to him by the Penney headquarters, but he chooses what he wants. He is not required to accept any items that he feels are not suitable for his own locality.

In short, he runs his store on a completely decentralized basis as if it were his very own, with nothing more than gentle policy guidance from the top. His only requirement is to run the store at a profit.

So remember that as a manager, you will demonstrate faith in your subordinates when you give them the authority to do the job along with the responsibility of doing it. Do that and you'll increase their desires to accept more and greater responsibilities.

Back His Decisions—Let Him Put His Methods to Work

If you want your people to assume responsibility for what they do, you must back them and support their actions. If your employee feels that he doesn't have your backing, he isn't about to stick his neck out for you with new ideas, bold solutions, or unorthodox methods—for fear he'll get his head chopped off.

But if your employee knows you'll back his decisions and

support his actions, he can then devote all his energies to doing his job in the best way he knows how.

"Taking the blame for someone else's mistakes takes a lot of guts," says Henry Mahoney, Shipping Department Supervisor for Merck & Company, Inc., of Rahway, New Jersey. "It's tough enough to be blamed by the boss for your own mistakes, but when you get chewed out for what someone else does, it's hard to swallow. But there's no other way if you want your people to really put out for you, make decisions on their own, and accept complete responsibility for what they do."

I don't know of any other way, either. If you're going to be a top-notch manager—if you want your employees to assume more responsibility—if you expect to get things done through people—you'll simply have to back their decisions and support their actions to the fullest.

Hold Him Accountable for Results

When we talk about responsibility and authority, there is one more word that must be considered: *accountability*. They are all equally important in your management of people.

For instance, your people must know what their responsibilities are—what authority they have—and they must also understand that they will be held accountable to you. Unless this last part is fully understood, you'll not be able to get the results that you want.

"All employees in our company—and there are no exceptions—must be ready to account for the results of their daily work," says Fred L. Owens, Director of Loss Prevention Services for the Fleetwood Corporation, manufacturer of fine quality mobile homes, travel trailers, and motor homes. "If the results are unfavorable and are not properly accounted for, then corrective action must be taken by supervision.

"It is imperative, though, that before you give anyone responsibility, he must know what his authority is. Only then can you properly hold him strictly accountable for the results.

"This principle applies to all areas in our company: production, safety and accident prevention, quality, cost control, executive management, etc. If any single supervisor is afraid to hold one of his people accountable for results, then he must be ready to explain, and if necessary, to accept the consequences for their failures. He, too, is held responsible. This is a requirement of ours at all levels of management and supervision from the top to the bottom. There are no exceptions."

This is effective management. It gets results. If you have lower standards than these, you may get lots of activity in your organization, but not necessarily results.

A great many supervisors hesitate to take corrective action when they should. They don't like to hold people accountable for their mistakes. They're managers in name only.

In conclusion, then, let me say that your people must have a clear understanding of what is expected from them. They must know what their responsibilities are and what authority they have. Then you must hold them strictly accountable for their actions. If mistakes are made, correct them without hesitation. When you do, you'll get results.

SEVENTEEN

Emphasizing Rules Rather Than Skill

"What's the matter, Sam?" I said as my letter carrier handed me my morning mail. "You really look down in the mouth today. Come to think of it, I haven't seen you now for about a week. You been sick?"

"No, I haven't been sick, Jim," he said. "I was suspended for five days and fined a hundred dollars besides."

"Holy cow, Sam, that's rough just before Christmas," I said. "What in the world did you do?"

"Well, you know I live on this route, Jim. In fact, I deliver mail to my own house, so I've been going home for lunch. My schedule calls for me to eat at 11 o'clock, but when the mail's light, I wait until I get everything delivered before I eat. Some days when I'm through real early I've been spending from an hour to an hour and a half at home. But if I didn't do that, I'd just have to go back in and sit around the post office doing absolutely nothing.

"I guess somebody saw my jeep over there and reported it. Anyway, the postmaster rapped me with a suspension and a fine for all sorts of 'crimes,' like misuse of a government vehicle, not keeping my proper schedule, eating at the wrong time and place, taking too much time to eat, not being at the right place on my route, and so on."

"Didn't you tell him all your mail was delivered, Sam?" I said.

"Sure I did, but he said I couldn't spend that time at home.

Have to come back to the post office and wait until my eight hours are up."

"Well, is there anything you could do back there . . . work of any sort, say like getting ready for the next day?" I said.

"Heck, no, Jim. If I went ahead and cased my mail ahead of time, I'd be through that much earlier tomorrow," Sam said. "And my route book is spotless. Can't do a thing to improve it. I post everything up to date each morning before I leave.

"No, Jim, when I go back early I just have to sit around and kill time until my eight hours are up before I can punch out. I loaf in the carriers' lounge, drink coffee, read a book, watch TV, play pinochle, anything at all to pass time. The postmaster doesn't care what we do as long as we do it in the lounge where nobody else can see us, I guess."

"Is every day like this, Sam?" I said. "I'd think they'd lengthen your route and add some more stops to it."

"No, I don't end up early every day," Sam said. "Like some days when we carry a lot of junk mail I'd have to work overtime to get it all delivered. That's why the inspector won't add any more houses to my route. But they won't let us work overtime anyway. Makes the postmaster look bad. So on extra-heavy days they have a substitute carrier handle part of my route."

"Have you ever suggested a different system of delivery, Sam?" I said. "You know, I was thinking, like, work seven hours one day when you have a short load and nine hours the next day when you have a heavy load. That way you could end up with 40 hours a week, not have to worry about overtime, and still get the job done."

"Sure I have, Jim," Sam said. "But when you go over eight hours a day you have to be paid overtime, so they won't let you do that. I'd love that system. Then I could work until I was done and quit. The faster I work, the quicker I'd be through. But they won't do it that way.

"I've even suggested they work out a mail delivery system that would pay the carrier on an incentive basis, like so much for every house you deliver mail to. Here again, if you walk fast like I do and push hard, you could make more money for yourself, but it'd still cost the post office less. That way, a carrier would get paid for the actual work he does, not just for the hours he puts in. But they turned that idea down, too.

"It's no use, Jim; they won't listen to new ideas. I've got 12 years in with the post office, so I'll just have to do what the postmaster says. He told me not to walk so fast so I wouldn't get through so early. 'Course, you'll get your mail an hour later each day, but I can't help that."

No wonder the post office always operates at a deficit. Their only solution to increased operating costs is not to improve their methods, but always to raise the postage rates.

I wonder how many part-time letter carriers they could get rid of if they'd use Sam's method of quitting early on short-volume days and working longer to make up for it on heavy days. I also wonder what would happen if they'd put the carriers on an incentive basis; for instance, the more houses on the route, the higher the pay—that sort of thing.

What a contrast this picture of inefficient postal service is to the dynamic Skyline Corporation. The Skyline Corporation, one of the leading manufacturers of mobile homes, headquartered in Elkhart, Indiana, has 39 manufacturing and assembly plants scattered throughout the United States.

It's president, Arthur J. Decio, is only 41. He has led the company since he was 27. When he took over, annual sales were running $9.5 million. Today they run $252 million, more than 26 times what they were in the beginning.

Mr. Decio insists on, and gets, fast production from his well-paid workers, who are non-union, and much of whose pay depends on how much they turn out. Morale is high. Each plant has a long waiting list of men and women who want to work for Skyline even though it is non-union.

Skyline builds its homes only to order. Employees work until the day's quota—usually 17 or 18 mobile homes for each of the assembly plants across the country—is filled. Only then do they quit for the day. This doesn't necessarily mean a long day. In fact, it can mean a short one, for if they're fast, they may leave early.

Employees police their own ranks for those who don't produce as they should. Not only do they get rid of people who are slow or lazy, but they also eliminate the man who tries to short-cut and skip necessary production steps in an attempt to speed up the assembly process. They know if quality falls off, they will lose the privilege of quitting early and still getting paid for a full day's work.

Are Mr. Decio's methods effective? They sure are. *Skyline is number one in dollar sales* of the 400 builders in the mobile housing industry. *It is also number one in the number of units manufactured.* Among the country's 500 largest corporations, *it is number one for return on shareholders' equity. It is also completely debt-free, which again earns it a number one rating.*

Why is it number one in all these areas? Well, first of all, because Mr. Decio emphasizes skill rather than rules. He believes in cutting through the fat of a problem to get to its heart. His favorite saying is, "If you make it good, now make it better."

When you emphasize skill rather than rules just as Mr. Decio does . . .

YOU'LL GAIN THESE BENEFITS

1. You can concentrate on results—not methods.
2. Production and/or sales will go up.
3. Costs and expenses will go down.
4. You'll attract a better class of employees.
5. Your employees will put their initiative to work for you.
6. They'll give you their maximum efforts.
7. Employee morale and esprit de corps will be high.
8. You'll have fewer management-labor problems.
9. You, too, can become number one.

TECHNIQUES YOU USE TO GAIN THESE BENEFITS

Give Him a Job to Do—Then Let Him Do It

Judge a man's actions by the results he gets—not by the methods he uses. Your primary interest should be in terms of increasing the competitive position of your company and the satisfaction of the basic human needs and desires of your employees.

So go easy on the pat rules. Don't insist that they always do it by the book. That isn't always the best way. If an unorthodox solution works just as well and pleases the man who uses it, then there's no reason to stop him just because his method is different.

Just as long as the five main managerial resources of men,

money, material, time, and facilities are being used in such a way as to get the *maximum results,* you shouldn't care at all how the job is done—as long as it's done the best way possible.

A few years ago I told the following true story in my book, *Guide to Managing People.** Many of my readers have written to say how much they liked it, and since over the years I've never found a better example to illustrate this technique, I'm going to repeat it here for your benefit.

No Accidents—No Lectures!

The commander of Kadena Air Base in Okinawa, a full bird colonel, was in hot water with his superiors because of the high accident rate on his base. In the daily chewing-out session of his base safety officer, the colonel made it clear that unless this situation improved rapidly, the base safety officer was going to be out of a job—not just as safety officer, but in the entire air force!

In a frenzy of activity, the safety officer scheduled safety lectures almost every hour. Safety films were shown in the theaters instead of the latest movies fresh from the states. These were shown during the most accident-prone part of the week—Saturday and Sunday afternoons and evenings. Compulsory attendance? Naturally!

Passes and leaves were cancelled. Airmen were restricted to the base; drivers' licenses were revoked and suspended. Every precaution was taken to prevent an accident. The base was living in a sea of safety slogans; they were plastered on every wall. The command was knee-deep in a veritable flood of lectures; millions of words on safety had been spoken. The safety officer had followed every possible rule in the book, but the accidents kept right on happening!

Then, close to a state of panic himself, the colonel relieved the safety officer and appointed the newest second lieutenant from the states to the job. That young officer, a fighter pilot anxious to be in the air over the East China Sea on patrol duty, was disgusted with this ground assignment. The commander assured him that as soon as the crisis was over he would be immediately restored to flying duty.

---

* From the book *Guide to Managing People* by James K. Van Fleet, © 1968 by Parker Publishing Company, Inc., West Nyack, New York.

In less than one week the lieutenant was back in the colonel's office; twenty-four hours after he'd taken over, the accidents had completely stopped. The rate was down to zero.

"How in the world did you do it?" the colonel asked, astounded at the lieutenant's performance.

"Simple, sir," the lieutenant said. "I figured if the safety officer had been going by the rules, the rules must be wrong. So I stopped everything he'd been doing. I assembled all the men and held one meeting with them. It lasted less than thirty seconds. I spoke only five words. I said, 'Gentlemen, *no accidents—no lectures!*'"

Challenge Him to Beat Your System

Most men will rise to a challenge just as a boy will refuse to turn down a dare. It's a matter or pride. If someone tells you that you can't do it, chances are you'll go all out to prove that he's wrong.

Incentive plans in business and industry work on the same principle. Wage incentive plans on a production line in a factory work for the employee just like a salary plus commission for a salesman. The wage incentive system stimulates a man's thinking. It forces him to use his initiative to beat you at your own game.

Once a quota is set and a standard of performance is fixed for the average individual's work, then your employees will use their ingenuity and their skills to beat your system. They'll produce more so you'll have to pay them more incentive pay.

The procedure used by Mr. Decio, President of the Skyline Corporation, is also an incentive plan. However, it would be classified more as a *time incentive plan* than a wage incentive plan. As you've already seen (remember Skyline is number one in a lot of ways), his methods work.

So if you can't afford to pay a man on a wage incentive system, consider the time incentive plan. Or if you're a department foreman or a section supervisor, suggest the procedure to your boss. You could be well rewarded yourself, for such a plan is one of the biggest morale boosters I've ever seen. Money is important to a person, but so is time off, and I've seen people work harder to beat the system for some extra free time than for extra money.

Whichever way you go, remember that the principle is basically the same. When you challenge a man to beat your system—whether it be for time off or money or both—you're appealing to his sense of pride. So when all else fails you, throw down a challenge. Nearly everyone will rise to the occasion.

Let Him Improve His Own Job Methods

A good way to emphasize skill instead of rules is to let each person figure out ways to improve his own job methods. Of course, if you're using a wage incentive system or a time incentive plan, this step will become almost automatic.

It's to your own benefit if you can show a person how to improve the way he does his job. If you can help him beat your system, you're that much better off; that's what you wanted in the first place.

"We try to help our employees beat the company," says Joe Gammon, head of the Time and Motion Study Section in the Industrial Engineering Department of Western Electric's Kansas City plant. "If they can figure out a simpler way to do their job faster so they can make more money, so much the better. We're all for that. After all, the more money they make for themselves, the more they make for Western Electric.

"So we try to help a man simplify his job and improve his work methods ourselves. For instance, we give him a card with four questions to be answered about his job. This is certainly no magic formula, but it does help him organize his thinking. Here's what the card looks like:

HOW TO IMPROVE YOUR JOB METHODS

One of the biggest time killers on your job can be unnecessary steps taken in doing things. The answer? Simplify your job procedures. Don't know where to start? You can begin by answering these four questions about the way you now do your job.

1. *What are the separate steps I use in doing my job?* Actually put them down in writing so you can study them.

2. *Can any of these steps be skipped without spoiling the results?* Many times, we become habit-bound and

keep on doing things just because we've always done them that way. Check every step in your job and see if any of them can be gotten rid of.

3. *Can I change the order of these steps?* Just because you've always done your work XYZ doesn't mean that ZYX might not be better.

4. *Are there any details on my job that ought to be done by someone else?* Review your work and see if there are any time-consuming details you are now doing that actually should be done by someone else.

"Of course, this doesn't help a man solve all his job problems, nor does it put the time and motion study section out of business. But it does help him channel his thinking in the right direction. He can try to improve his work methods in a systematic, organized manner, and that's what we're really after."

How to Emphasize Skill By Making Effective Rules

In discussing how to avoid the mistake of emphasizing rules rather than skill, it is almost inevitable that we should talk about how to make rules that emphasize skill so people will be glad to follow them.

In most organizations managers formulate and administer the rules for their employees. They dictate what is proper and what is improper for their people to do. Top management arbitrarily sets the rules. It then becomes the job of the foreman or supervisor to enforce them and for the rank-and-file subordinate to follow them.

However, experience has shown that once the people of a department decide for themselves what rules should apply to their own activities, they will enforce their own rules much more effectively than they will the supervisor's rules under the so-called traditional system. Remember how the Skyline Corporation's employees police their own ranks?

In spite of this lesson of experience, I'm sure your organization operates in the traditional way of management making the rules for employees to follow. And since I'm also inclined to doubt if any drastic changes are going to be made in that procedure, I do want to recommend that you at least make some reasonable rules that will emphasize skill. Then your people will want to follow them. For that reason I've included here some . . .

TECHNIQUES YOU CAN USE FOR
EFFECTIVE RULE-MAKING

1. When you make rules, concentrate on results to be obtained—not methods to be used.
2. A good rule will consider the health, safety, and welfare of your employees.
3. A good rule will help to increase production and sales —to decrease costs and expenses.
4. Your people should be stimulated by your rules to use their initiative and to give you their best efforts possible.
5. Good rules should improve employee morale and esprit de corps.
6. They should improve a man's individual proficiency on the job.
7. They should also raise your overall organizational efficiency.
8. Good rules should reduce management-labor problems.

If any rule that you're about to put into practice won't bring you at least one of the above benefits, you'd better check it over again. Chances are, something's wrong with it.

EIGHTEEN

Failing to Keep Your Criticism Constructive

A good many years ago I went to work as a shift supervisor in a rubber factory. The young department foreman who was to be my boss had been having all sorts of problems with his people.

Production had fallen off. Product rejection by the quality control section had gone up. So had spoilage and waste in his department. Morale was low; his men were surly, belligerent, and uncooperative. He was worried about losing his own job.

"I want you supervisors to write someone up on every single shift," he told us. "You can always get somebody for something. That's easy enough to do. The way they've been making mistakes and goofing off, you won't have any trouble at all finding a man to give a Step 4 to. Just keep your eyes open; you can always find something wrong somewhere. I don't care how you do it . . . just do it. I want you to scare hell out of 'em!"

"But what if we don't see anyone making a mistake?" I asked. "What do we do then?"

"Then make something up!" the young foreman yelled, slamming his fist down on the desk. "Damn it, I want you to let 'em know who's boss around here. Put the fear of God in 'em. Let 'em know they're not going to get by with anything any more!"

I know that the foreman wanted good production without mistakes; he wanted top performance from his people. He wanted results. These were the benefits he wanted to gain from his criticism, but he never got them. He simply went about it the wrong way. He's been long gone from that job for many years now, and so have I, but we left for far different reasons.

You'll not gain any lasting benefits whenever you threaten a person and try to use fear as a persuasive force. To make a man afraid, to threaten him with reduced earnings, loss of his status, his job, or his personal dignity and self-esteem cannot possibly bring any benefits to you. Unwarranted or destructive criticism will kill a person's initiative, his morale, and his desire to cooperate with you and help you.

No one likes to be criticized. No one likes to be told that he's wrong—that he's made a mistake. Even justified criticism has the potential power to destroy a good employee.

This is not to say that you should never criticize a person, but you should know how and when to do so. There'll be times when you have no other choice; you'll have no other way out. Not only that—not to criticize or to overlook a mistake is sometimes even worse than to do so. But your criticism must be both necessary and constructive. And it must benefit you, too, or it's a complete waste of time.

So before you criticize anyone, you ought to sit down and figure out what it is you're after . . . what it is that you want. In short, ask yourself what . . .

BENEFITS YOU CAN GAIN FROM YOUR CRITICISM

From experience I have found that the benefits I want to gain from constructive criticism of others are:

1. Peak performance,
2. Peak production (or sales),
3. Peak profits.

Production, performance, and profits should be your goals, too, when you criticize your people. If your criticism will bring you one of these benefits, you're on the right track; go ahead and criticize. But if it won't bring you any of these benefits, stop right there. Something's wrong; don't criticize.

TWELVE QUESTIONS YOU CAN ASK YOURSELF
TO ACHIEVE THESE BENEFITS

1. When Something Goes Wrong, Do You Tend to Assume Who's at Fault?

In the factory where I worked so long ago they had a problem employee named Bill. Whenever a supervisor went in to the office to report a problem or an incident of some sort, the foreman would always say, in effect, "What's Bill up to now" or "What's Bill done this time?"

But Bill wasn't really such a bad sort at all. He'd just got off to a poor start with the foreman and his supervisor, and from then on they blamed him for everything that went wrong.

Finally Bill got tired of being accused of every crime, so he began to create real trouble for them: all kinds and lots of it. He was at the bottom of all sorts of schemes to slow down production. He falsified his incentive reports, filed all kinds of phony grievances; in fact, he did everything he could do to harass management and drive them crazy. As he told me, "If they're always going to accuse me of being at the bottom of everything, then they might as well get their money's worth!"

Don't make the mistake of accusing someone before you know who's at fault. Just as it's important to give credit to the right person for doing a job properly, it's also important to criticize the right man when something goes wrong. You must always be sure to pin the tail on the right donkey. Pin it on the wrong one often enough and he'll kick you, too.

2. Do You Do Your Best to Get All the Facts First?

Along this same line, you ought to get all your facts straight before you jump on someone. Don't be like the manager who says, "My mind's already made up—don't confuse me with facts."

Don't accept hearsay or rumors as factual evidence. Be specific. Find out *who* did or *who* said *what, when, where,* and *why.* One thing that always gets to me is to be told, "*They* said . . . *they* told me . . . that's the way *they* want it." I want to know specifically *who* said . . . *who* told . . . *who* wants it done that way.

I would like to say here that if you can't get all the facts you need to determine who is at fault or who should be punished, don't make the mistake so many army officers make of punishing everybody when they can't find the guilty person. Everyone will resent you for that.

I've forgotten the names of all the generals who commanded the divisions I served in during World War II except for one, General Lucius B. Hart. How could I forget him? He restricted the entire 44th Division to the post for the weekend just because he couldn't get all the answers about a disturbance in one of his regiments.

Oh yes, I remember him extremely well—for I spent Friday, Saturday, and Sunday night in the barracks while my wife (whom I hadn't seen for six long months) waited for me in vain in a Tacoma, Washington, hotel room.

3. Do You Make Clear to the Person His Specific Offense?

Let the person know exactly what he has done wrong. Be specific. Don't talk in generalities or refuse to go into details with him. One of the reasons you're criticizing the person is to achieve the benefit of improved performance. To get that benefit, you must tell him what he's doing wrong so he can keep from doing it again.

Many school teachers make this mistake. One day when my daughter was in the third grade, she came home in tears. Nothing would stop her crying. Finally we got the story out of her.

In one of her classes they'd been making Easter baskets. A young substitute teacher was there that day. She would walk up and down the aisle telling the children whether their work was good or bad. Unfortunately, that's as far as she went. She didn't tell them why their work was good or where their mistakes were.

When she reached my daughter's desk, she looked down and said, "Oh, Teresa, that's absolutely no good at all." Naturally, my daughter was crushed. Not only was her work wrong, but now she didn't know what to do about it—she didn't know how to correct it.

You think managers are any different than teachers? Some are, but most aren't. If you catch yourself saying, "You haven't got the right attitude . . . that's all wrong . . . you're always messing things up . . . that's no good . . . you should be more careful," and then stop with that, chances are you're exactly like that substitute teacher.

So when you do criticize a man's work, make his specific mistakes extremely clear to him so he can correct them. Make certain he knows exactly what you're criticizing. Otherwise, you're wasting your time.

4. Do You Control Your Temper When You're Criticizing a Person?

Don't act while you're angry. Be completely calm, rational, and as objective as you can be when you're criticizing someone. Don't let it turn into an old-fashioned chewing-out or a tongue-lashing. A few *nevers* you can keep in mind to help you control your temper are these:

Never raise your voice. Keep a purely conversational tone and voice level. The moment you raise your voice, your subordinate tends to do the same. Soon you'll have nothing but a shouting match, with each one of you trying to drown out the other.

Never use profanity. It's all too easy to go from "damn it!" to "damn you!"—and then all is lost. You've lost your dignity as a manager, you've insulted your subordinate and alienated him completely and permanently.

Never act in haste. Give yourself some time to cool off before calling the person into your office. Then you're calm and collected. So is he. You can face each other sensibly and rationally discuss what happened, and take steps to keep it from happening again.

5. Do You Always Talk Things Over in Private?

"I learned early in this game not to criticize a man in front of others," says Earl S. Pearce, Industrial Relations Manager for the Barracuda Boat Corporation of Miami, Florida. "To reprimand a man in the presence of his associates or his fellow workers causes humiliation and resentment rather than a desire to do better in the future. Orientals aren't the only ones who hate to lose face.

"To criticize a man in front of others undermines his morale, his self-confidence, and his desire to do his best for you. It's embarrassing, not only to him, but also to those around him.

"I criticize when I must only on a face-to-face basis, behind closed doors, completely in private, away from prying eyes and eager ears. You can't do it any other way if you want to get the best results."

That's so true. You can't do it any other way if you want to get the best results. A team of psychologists at Columbia University determined that in a survey they made. They divided a large number of volunteers into five groups and gave each group the same series of challenging jobs to do.

As each group finished its work, it was briefed on its performance, but in different ways. For example, the first group was *criticized openly in front of others*. The second group was *criticized individually in private*. Then the groups performed the same work again.

In the group that was criticized in public, only 34 percent improved their performance. But in the group criticized in private, 66 percent, or *nearly twice as many*, did better the second time.

The lesson to be learned here should be crystal clear to you. *When you do criticize, do it in private.*

6. Do You Praise Before You Criticize?

Always begin your interview with sincere praise and honest admiration. Don't blast a man through the wall the moment he comes into your office. Don't list all his defects one after another from a prepared list. Few people can take that kind of punishment.

Tell him how good he is, how much you think of him, how lucky you are to have him as an employee, what a good job he's actually been doing—*except for this one small point you want to talk over with him* so he can make his performance even better.

The third group tested by the psychologists at Columbia University was handled even differently than the first two. This group was criticized in private, as was the second group. But before the members of this group were criticized, *they were praised.*

The result? On the second time around, *88 percent im-*

proved their performance. This is an increase of 24 percent over the second group, who received private criticism without praise. If you'll remember, 66 percent of that group did better the second time.

So keep this point in mind, if you will, the next time you call someone in for a counselling session. It'll pay you dividends, for everyone hungers for a word of praise. Everyone likes a compliment. As Mark Twain once said, "I could live for two months on one good compliment."

Praise first—criticize next—praise again at the end. Try it; you can't miss. Results are guaranteed.

7. Do You Share Responsibility for the Man's Mistakes?

An excellent way to take some of the sting out of your criticism is to accept at least part of the blame for his mistake. That makes him feel you're on his side. For instance, you could say, "Perhaps I didn't make myself completely clear on that, Sam . . . evidently you misunderstood exactly what I wanted, Joe. . . ."

Then make sure that he does understand exactly what you want, or that he reads you loud and clear so there'll be no possibility of another mistake like that.

Another good way to include yourself in the responsibility is to use the preposition *we.* For example, you could say, *"We've* never had any trouble with your machine before, Sam. What happened?" "This is the first accident like this *we've* had around here, Joe. What went wrong?" *"We* almost never misroute an order here in town, George. How come?"

Whatever you do or however you do it, just remember you'll make his criticism a lot easier to stomach if you share the responsibility with him for his mistakes.

8. Do You Listen to His Side of the Story, Too?

Give a man plenty of chance to talk. If you don't, you'll probably never find out what really happened and you won't be able to help him correct his mistake.

Most people are extremely anxious to let you know what happened. They want to make sure you understand their side of it and most of them will talk without much pushing from you.

If a man does seem reluctant to open up, ask him some leading questions. Give him the opportunity to unload all his problems and you should be able to uncover the real reason for his mistake. And there may be mitigating circumstances, conflicting orders, perhaps even instructions you gave that were not clear enough to him.

At any rate, take the time to listen to his side of it. You'll be in a much better position to help him—and yourself, too—by taking the proper corrective action to keep this mistake from happening again.

9. Do You Allow a Person to Retain His Dignity?

You should never ridicule a person, use sarcasm, or belittle him. Don't make comments like "How stupid can you get, Ed? How dumb can you be, Joe? What a bonehead stunt to pull, Sam!"

When you do this, you're not criticizing the act—you're criticizing the person. Tell him what's wrong with his work—not what's wrong with him.

Those Columbia University psychologists also found out some other interesting points in their survey. They found that when private ridicule and sarcasm were used after the first performance, only 17 percent improved on the second try. When the group was exposed to public ridicule and sarcasm, only 11 percent responded with a better performance the second time.

Look back at those other figures and you can quickly see that it will pay you dividends when you help a person retain his dignity and his self-esteem by not ridiculing him or making fun of him.

10. Do You Suggest Specific Steps to Prevent Reoccurrence of the Mistake?

Tell the person exactly what he can do to improve his performance. That's the purpose of the exercise. Unless you include that in your criticism, you've probably wasted your time. Then follow up to make sure he does carry out your suggestions.

William J. Thornton, President of Thornton & Associates, an Atlanta, Georgia, management consulting firm, says, "If you were to ask me why criticism is often ineffective, I would tell you that most of the time no follow-up is made. It's easy to put a man on the carpet and then forget all about him until he makes the next mistake. If you want to get the most mileage out of your criticism, follow up to make sure you get the results you're after."

11. Do You Keep Accurate Records?

Disciplinary records must always be kept in the personnel folder of the person. This will become part of his work history and will furnish evidence if further disciplinary action, especially dismissal, is taken.

For instance, reprimands are often termed "Steps," and are numbered from 1 through 4. The first disciplinary action will be the mildest one, a Step 4. If he repeats, the next time you'd give him a Step 3. But if you failed to file the Step 4 in his personnel folder, you're stuck. You have to start all over from the bottom again.

I have seen many instances where people who were known to be unsatisfactory employees have been reinstated by a federal arbitrator after being discharged by the company, simply because management could not produce the necessary evidence to prove the person had been told about his shortcomings.

Don't let it happen to you. If you keep accurate records, it won't.

12. Do You Forgive and Forget?

You must, if you want to be an effective manager. Sure you have to record a reprimand in his personnel folder, but that doesn't mean you should carry his file around in your hip pocket and whip it on him every time he looks at you cross-eyed.

Once the reprimand has been given and the punishment rendered, don't walk around with a chip on your shoulder looking for trouble. The person required discipline and he received it. He paid the penalty. Now let him start with a clean slate; give him the second chance.

In Summary, Then . . .

To determine if your own criticism is constructive or not, answer these questions—most of which we've already discussed —for yourself.

1. When something goes wrong, do you tend to assume who is at fault?
2. Do you do your best to get all the facts first?
3. Do you talk down to the person who's at fault?
4. Do you make clear to the person his specific offense?
5. Do you control your temper when criticizing a person?
6. Do you always talk things over in private?
7. Do you praise before you criticize?
8. Do you share responsibility for the mistake?
9. Do you feel there are times when only an old-fashioned chewing-out will get results?
10. Do you listen to his side of the story, too?
11. Do you give ground even when you're right?
12. Do you try to scare a person by your criticism?
13. Do you allow a person to retain his dignity?
14. Do you suggest specific steps to prevent reoccurence?
15. Do you keep accurate records of your counselling sessions?
16. Do you forgive and forget?

Let me wrap this up by saying that this list of questions is not final, nor is it all-inclusive. That would be impossible, for no two people or two situations are ever completely alike.

It should serve, however, as a basis for you to make your own criticism constructive. You may have other areas you need to work on and other guidelines you want to add. Please do so. If I have at least headed you in the right direction, then I have done what I set out to do.

NINETEEN

Not Paying Attention to Employee Gripes and Complaints

The other day I read an article in the evening paper that said, "Employees of the 3M Company, 3211 East Trafficway in Springfield, Missouri, yesterday again defeated a bid by the International Brotherhood of Allied Pottery Workers to unionize the plant.

" 'Last year, the bid was rejected by 66 percent of our people,' the local plant manager, Mr. Leon Skelly, said. 'This year, even more of our employees voted against bringing the union in to represent them; 75 percent of our people said they didn't want it.' "

I was quite surprised to read this, knowing that the usual way for employees to work out their problems with management is to organize into a labor union so they can have more bargaining power and be represented by a unanimous voice in presenting their demands to the company.

So I got permission from the plant manager to interview some of his employees to find out why they had voted against unionizing the plant.

"How come?" I asked. "Is it because they pay higher wages than union plants? Do they offer you better benefits?"

"It's because they treat us like human beings," one man said. "They listen to our problems. They pay attention to our complaints."

"That's right," a woman spoke up. "That's the main reason, I think. They listen to what we have to say and they do something about it. They treat us as if we're important members of the company—not just pieces of machinery. I worked for a rubber factory before I came here and I was never treated as decently as I am now. Just the opposite, in fact, and I was in the union over there."

And that was the general consensus. They didn't need a union because management already had a good grievance procedure. They helped their employees solve their problems. They listened to their people. They paid attention to their gripes and their complaints.

Now I also knew that nearly two thousand production employees of the Lily-Tulip Company in Springfield—one of the world's largest manufacturers of paper and plastic cups, containers, dishes, and cartons for food and drink vendors, hospitals, nursing homes, restaurants, cafeterias, and home use— had voted year after year since the spring of 1952 not to unionize. So while gathering information for this chapter, I got permission to visit their plant and talk to some of their people, too. I got the same sort of answers they gave me at 3M.

I also reviewed the notes I'd made during my visits to the Lincoln Electric Company in Cleveland, Ohio, several years ago. They never had any labor troubles there either, for every two weeks the president called a conference of labor and management, where employee problems were discussed.

If any employee had a complaint, he was urged and encouraged to attend these conferences and speak his piece. It should be especially noted that at these meetings the president, Mr. James F. Lincoln, insisted that management listen *so they could learn what their employees wanted.* The end result? Complete harmony. No labor problems; no strikes.

Do you want to find out what your own employees want? *Then listen to them with an open mind.* Do you want your people to do their best for you? *Then let them talk to you about their personal problems, their complaints, their worries, and their fears.* Do you want a man to level with you—to tell you the whole truth? *Then pay attention to him—give him the courtesy of listening to what he has to say.* To listen courteously and attentively is one of the highest compliments you can ever pay a man. When you do this . . .

YOU'LL GAIN THESE BENEFITS

You'll Get to Know and Understand Each Employee Better

What irritates a person can be a key to his personality. If he objects to reasonable rules and regulations, he may be a malcontent and a troublemaker. If you know this, you're way ahead of him. If, on the other hand, his complaints are usually justified and not too frequent, he's probably a well-adjusted individual. What genuinely disturbs a person should be taken into consideration in your assessment of his overall value to you.

When you know and understand each employee better, you'll not only find out what bothers him, but you'll also discover what turns him on. You can determine where his true interests lie—what his real value is to the company—how he can be motivated to do a better job for you.

Even Though You're Management, Your Employees Will Like You When You Listen

Oliver Wendell Holmes, Justice of the United States Supreme Court for 30 years, once said, "To be able to listen to others in a sympathetic and understanding manner is perhaps the most effective mechanism in the world for getting along with people and tying up their friendship for good."

It's just plain old human nature for your people to like you when you listen to them attentively. Let me ask you this: Have you yourself ever disliked a person who listened attentively to your ideas and your opinions? Or let me say it another way: Have you ever really liked someone who wouldn't listen to you? See what I mean?

Your People Will Know You're Really Interested in Them

I know of no faster way to turn a person off than to pay no attention to him or to his problems. By the same token, you can turn him on when you show how interested you really are in him and in what he says. A good way to show your interest is to ask questions like "What did you do then?" "What happened after that?" "What did you say next?"

Even the most reluctant and bashful person will open up

and talk when you show your interest in him this way. So concentrate 100 percent on what he is saying. Focus all your attention on him. Listen to him with all the intensity and awareness you can command.

You'll Find Out What Your Employees Really Want When You Listen to Them

People will tell you what they really want from you if you'll just take the time to listen to them. So forget yourself and what you want from them for a change. Concentrate completely on what they want from you and what you can do for them.

"Finding out what people want and helping them get it is the most important secret of salesmanship," says Frank Bettger in his book, *How I Raised Myself from Failure to Success in Selling.** Mr. Bettger is a super salesman. In fact, he became one of the most successful salesmen this country has ever produced.

"People will tell you what they want from you if you'll just listen," says Les Giblin in his book, *How to Have Confidence and Power in Dealing with People.*** Mr. Giblin is a master of the art of effective human relations.

So take the word of two top-notch professionals. You, too, can gain the benefit of finding out what people really want so you can help them get it and help yourself at the same time when you do so. All you have to do to get started out on the right track is simply *listen to them.*

TECHNIQUES YOU CAN USE TO GAIN THESE BENEFITS

Listening to Problems Is a Manager's Responsibility

Perhaps you think you shouldn't have to listen to an employee's complaints. After all, you tell yourself, you're too busy with your own problems: cutting costs, meeting quotas and deadlines, increasing production, improving quality, attending meetings. Not only that, you say that's why your company has an industrial relations manager, a personnel section to handle gripes, an employee relations counselor—so your people can go

---

* Frank Bettger, *How I Raised Myself from Failure to Success in Selling* (Englewood Cliffs, New Jersey: Prentice-Hall, Inc., 1949).
** Les Giblin, *How to Have Confidence and Power in Dealing with People,* (Englewood Cliffs, New Jersey: Prentice-Hall, Inc., 1956).

to them with their complaints about pay or working conditions, or whatever.

"Not true," says George Wilson, Employee Relations Manager with Chrysler's automobile assembly plant in St. Louis, Missouri. "Listening to the complaints and gripes of an employee is one of the most important responsibilities every single supervisor has.

"The employee relations department is the company's final line of defense. It's where the last ditch effort is made to satisfy an unhappy employee who's got a beef with the company. If we can't satisfy him, his complaint will probably become a formal grievance to be filed by the union with management.

"Every attempt should be made to take care of a complaint at the lowest possible level. The person's immediate supervisor is most familiar with the problem and he should try to come up with a satisfactory answer. If he can't, then he should go to his foreman for help in solving his subordinate's problem.

"Here in our plant, when a man comes to our office with a complaint, we want his immediate supervisor to come with him. In fact, when the problem can't be solved at a lower level, we expect the supervisor to take the initiative in bringing the employee to see us.

"That's what we like to see happen. However, it's not an ironclad rule and it doesn't always work that way. So our door is always open to any employee who has a complaint—with or without his supervisor.

"I can usually tell what's wrong when an employee comes in by himself to see me. His supervisor thinks he's too busy or too important to listen to the man's troubles. When too many people show up from the same department with complaints, I know the real problem doesn't lie with the employees—it's their section chief, their foreman or supervisor, who's at fault."

How to Be a Good Listener

There are a few better ways to raise morale, to win the regard and respect, to gain the maximum effort from others, than to really listen to their gripes and their complaints. To pay close attention to a man's problems shows you are really interested in him, that you respect him, that you feel he does have something worthwhile to tell you.

"The manager who knows his people best listens to their complaints," says Dwight Austin, production technical foreman for the Firestone Company's Orange, Texas, branch. "He has to; otherwise, he wouldn't be able to really know them. I encourage my people to talk by asking them questions about themselves, their families, their outside interests, their work, what they don't like about the company, what they do like about us.

"The only sure way to actually learn what makes a man tick—and why—is to give him your undivided attention so you can really listen to what he says. This is especially true when he's presenting a complaint to you."

To be an effective listener means you must use great patience. I know there'll be times when you'll be so busy that you think, *just one more complaint from someone and I'll blow my cool!* And that's exactly when another one of your people will come to you with a personal problem.

Now this problem of his may not seem like much to you at all, but it's the most important thing at that moment to your employee, or he wouldn't have come to you for help. So ask him to sit down and talk it over with you. You may have to get him started off, but get him to talk his problem out; let him get it off his chest. Many times he'll discover his own solution simply by talking about it with another person.

True enough, this could even take up some of your off-duty time, but it's a must if you want to have a smooth-running organization. Remember, an employee can't possibly function properly on the job for you when something's bothering him or when he's worrying about some personal problem.

How to Turn an Angry Employee into a Satisfied One Just by Listening.

As I said just a moment ago, listening to a man's complaints is a definite function and responsibility of a manager. To be able to do it properly takes a lot of skill and know-how. Roy Feldman, a top employee relations man at American Motors, has that know-how.

"When an angry employee comes through my door with a complaint, I handle him like a VIP," Roy says. "I treat him as if he were the president of the company or a majority stockholder. I have him sit down. I make him comfortable, give him a cigar, get him a cup of coffee. I do everything I can to put him at ease.

"After he's settled down, I ask him to tell me his story. I tell him I want to hear it all from beginning to end. *I listen to what he says without interrupting him or saying a single word.* That's the first thing he wants—someone who'll listen to him—someone who'll lend a sympathetic ear to his problem.

"When he's through, *I tell him I can sure understand how he feels.* I say that if I were in his position, if the situation were reversed, I'd probably feel the same way, too.

"Now I've already taken a lot of the steam out of him simply by listening to him and then by telling him I understand how he feels. He wasn't prepared for that, so he calms down even more. Instead of finding that I'm his enemy, he suddenly finds I'm his friend. He came in prepared to do battle with me, but now he finds he has no one to fight!

"*Next I ask him what he wants me to do about his complaint.* This really floors him because most of the time a manager doesn't *ask* his employee what he can do for him, he *tells* him what he's going to do.

"But we don't run our employee relations program that way. *We don't tell an employee with a complaint what we're going to do—we ask him what he wants us to do for him.*

"I've had men look at me in astonishment and say, 'Mr. Feldman, I honestly don't know. I hadn't thought about that. I just wanted someone to listen to my side of the story for a change. You've done that for me, so that's enough. I'm satisfied.'

"Sometimes they will tell me what they expect us to do. Ninety-five times out of a hundred, I find they ask for much less than I'd have offered them. Then when I give them more, they're really impressed with the generosity of both management and the company.

"Either way, when they leave, they're fully satisfied. You see, in both cases, they supplied themselves with their own answers, so they're bound to be completely happy with the end results.

"To tell the truth, my job is easy. All I do is listen. Then I ask what he wants me to do. When he tells me, I help him get what he wants."

Mr. Feldman's way of handling his employee relations job sounds a lot like Frank Bettger's method of *finding out what people want and helping them get it.* Evidently this important secret of salesmanship is also one of the secrets of how to get along with people so you can be a success in any field at all, no matter what it is.

One way you can make this method work for you as a manager is to set up a proper employee grievance procedure. To help you do this, here are . . .

TWELVE GUIDELINES YOU CAN USE TO IMPROVE YOUR HANDLING OF EMPLOYEE COMPLAINTS

1. *Make it easy for them to come to you.*   You don't have to be overly chummy, but you shouldn't be cold and distant with your people, either. However you do it, you must free your subordinate of the fear that stating his grievance will antagonize you. That's the important point.

2. *Get rid of red tape.*   Don't clutter up your grievance procedure with cumbersome rules and regulations. Keep it plain and simple. You want to get to the problem and its solution in the least possible time. A good way to do this is to keep an open door at all times.

3. *Explain your grievance procedure to everyone.*   It does no good to keep an open door for your employees unless they know it's open. So pass the word along—let them know—keep them all informed. State clearly how an employee should present his grievance and what will happen when he does, step by step.

4. *Help a person voice his own complaint.*   Sometimes an employee may be unskilled in putting his grievance into words. If he feels that the successful correction of his complaint will depend on his verbal ability, he may give up before he starts and bottle up his discontent.

5. *Always grant a hearing.*   No matter how trivial the complaint might seem to you, always grant the employee a hearing to air his gripe.

6. *Practice patience.*   I know you are busy and that you have many other things to do. But be patient; hear the man out. If you don't, chances are he'll go to the union with his complaint. The next time you see him it'll be in a formal arbitration hearing.

7. *Ask him what he wants you to do.*   This is how you can turn a complaint into a profitable session for you. This one

phrase can do much to oil any rusty relationships between management and labor.

8. *Don't render hasty or biased judgments.*   Even though you're a manager, make your decisions with the wisdom of a Solomon, not with the biased viewpoint of management. Nor should you make hasty or snap judgments. If you need more time to get more facts, do so. A wise decision is more important than a rapid one.

9. *Get all the facts.*   Sometimes you'll need to hear someone else's side of the story. If this is necessary to get all the facts, do so, no matter how much time it takes.

10. *Let him know what your decision is.*   Once you've made your decision, let him know what it is. Tell him yourself. Call him back into the office if need be. If you pass the word along by some secretary or some clerk, he'll know you weren't too interested after all.

11. *Double-check your results.*   Later on, check back with your employee to make sure the complaint has been taken care of to his complete satisfaction. Follow up and he'll know you're still interested.

12. *Be concerned.*   There's not much use of paying attention to a person and listening to his complaints unless you honestly do care about him, unless you really do want to help him, unless you won't feel right until you do. I can't tell you how to do this one; it has to come from inside.

I'm not for a moment implying that you can solve all the personal problems of your employees just by listening to their complaints, but paying close attention to them while they talk will help them and it will improve their attitude toward you and your company.

Doctor Paul Jansen, a Birmingham, Alabama, industrial pscyhologist, feels the same way. "You must pay attention to your employees and their problems if you want to help them," Dr. Jansen says. "I don't mean to give them your casual attention, either. *To pay means to part with something of value.* In this instance, that something of value is your time and your preoccupation with your own interests and desires.

"When you fail to pay attention to your employees and to listen to their problems and their complaints, you reject them. Rejection hurts. Attention heals. It's just that simple."

TWENTY

Failure to Keep Your People Informed

"I've found that most of our personnel problems here in the plant usually come from an employee not having enough information about what management has done and why," says Glen Ingersoll, Production Superintendent for the Kaiser Steel Corporation in Fontana, California. "It's important that you let a man know *what* you're going to do, *when, why,* and *how,* especially if your actions are going to affect him.

"For instance, just last week, one of our production employees was put out because it seemed as if a newer man had been promoted ahead of him. Of course, our company has a definite policy of promoting men of equal ability by seniority, so naturally, since Hank had been with us longer, he felt he'd been cheated.

"He filed a grievance with his shop steward and in less than 24 hours he received a full explanation that satisfied him. The man who'd been promoted had joined the company after Hank had, but before that he'd worked for more than six years for a company Kaiser Steel had bought out.

"One of the conditions of that purchase was that all members of that firm were to be credited for the years they'd worked there. As it turned out, the man who was promoted had two years seniority on Hank.

"Hank's complaint would never have been filed had he been given the proper information in the first place. That was my fault; I didn't pass the word along the way I should've. You can bet that everybody in the place has the full story now."

Ever been in the army? If you have, then I'm sure you've heard questions like these: "Why don't they let us know what's going on?" "Why don't they tell us what they want?" "Why do we always have to hurry up and wait?"

There's no reason for you to run your organization in such a way that your people have to ask you questions like that. *Every single employee of yours has the basic right to work and to think in the clear.* He shouldn't have to work and think in the dark.

He should be told the *why* and the *wherefore* of whatever he is expected to do, as well as the *what* and the *how*. His efficiency, morale, confidence, and enthusiasm will depend largely on how well you do that.

If you consistently brush off your subordinates, not keeping them properly informed just because you think your time is too valuable to spend any of it getting them on the right track, then you're doomed to work in an information vacuum yourself.

But if you believe in the importance of giving full information in a straightforward manner to your people and then you do exactly that, you'll get back much more than you give. In fact, when you do this . . .

YOU'LL GAIN THESE BENEFITS

You'll Encourage Their Initiative and Enthusiasm

If you want your people to do their best for you, keep them well informed about their individual progress. Each person wants to know what you expect from him. He also wants to know how well he has done—what you think of his work. He appreciates a word of praise and a pat on the back for a job well done.

If you keep your people well informed about their individual progress—if you let them know exactly where they stand with you—you'll encourage their initiative and enthusiasm. You'll improve their efficiency and raise their morale.

The Well-Informed Employee Is a Better Employee

The person who knows the big picture, who knows exactly how his own job fits in, who knows what you honestly think of him and his work, is a far better employee than one who's kept in the dark.

The well-informed employee is a more effective employee. He will have a positive attitude toward you and the organization. He can also understand what the company is doing and why it's doing it when he knows the long-range company objectives. A full understanding of the company's future goals will help him establish his own.

You'll Get Rid of Rumors

Keep your people informed and you'll get rid of vicious rumors that can cause a man to worry about his job security, a reduction in force, a loss in pay, no promotion, and the like.

To tell the plain truth is the only way to stop unfounded rumors and idle gossip. This act alone will automatically do away with many imagined conditions that can cause friction, misunderstanding, dissatisfaction, frustration, and fear among your employees.

You'll Gain a Man's Respect, Confidence, Willing Obedience, Loyal Cooperation, and Full Support

These are some tremendous dividends you can gain for yourself by the simple act of telling the truth and letting a man know what's honestly going on. But it's true. When you are open and frank with a man, when you tell him the straight truth, when you hide nothing from him, he will respect you and have confidence in you. He'll be willing to carry out your orders and do the job properly for you. He'll give you his loyal cooperation and full support.

TECHNIQUES YOU CAN USE TO GAIN THESE BENEFITS

Let People Know Exactly Where They Stand with You

"Most employees worry about what the boss thinks of them and the way they do their job, especially when he stands there and watches them work without saying a word," says Max Kilburn, Production Supervisor with the Occidental Chemical Company in Lathrop, California. "Don't you? Well, your subordinates are no different than you are.

"Try it sometime. Watch a man do his job. Don't say anything. Frown—look mean. Do you know what's going to happen? Your employee will start making mistakes. He can't help himself; he's worried. Even though you haven't said a single word, he's afraid the axe is about to fall simply because of the way you look at him.

"So I don't make my people guess. I don't play games with them. I tell them the truth; I level with them. If I think a man isn't doing his job properly, I tell him so. But if he's doing a good job, I let him know that, too. I find I can get even better results when I keep my people informed about their progress on the job."

Not only should you let a man know orally where he stands, just as Mr. Kilburn does, but you should also have some sort of performance review that will let you rate your employee periodically *in writing*. Keep a written record of how a man does his work. Let him see your written report and have him sign a statement saying he's read it. If you ever need to discharge someone for cause, you'll soon find out you need such documentation to prove your case.

To help you get started, here's a checklist I've used successfully over the years to rate people who've worked for me. If the person you're rating is in management—a supervisor, for instance—use the statements that are applicable to him and his job.

If the person is labor—a production employee, for example—you can do the same. This list is not final, by any means. You can add or delete items as you choose. You can also use it as the basis to make up a checklist of your own. (It's a good one to use to rate yourself, too.)

PERFORMANCE REVIEW CHECKLIST

1. Knows his job.
2. Can always be depended on.
3. Is preparing himself for advancement and promotion.
4. Looks for new ideas and supports worthwhile changes.
5. Accepts criticism gracefully from both above and below.
6. Is persistent—does not give up easily.

7. Sticks to major points—doesn't get lost on minor issues.
8. Is effective in "selling" his own ideas.
9. Resists pressures from below, above, outside.
10. Lets people know what they have to know—not what they want to know.
11. Is self-reliant.
12. Weighs the facts carefully and objectively.
13. Makes prompt decisions and sticks to them.
14. Makes allowances for human frailities.
15. Conducts himself by a proper code of ethics.
16. Keeps his head in an emergency.
17. Is respected by others.
18. Is an effective negotiator.

If You Don't Like a Man's Work, Tell Him So

You should not wait until it's time for a man's written performance review to let him know when you don't like the way he's doing his job. Let him know how you feel on a daily or weekly basis. Don't nag or harass; just tell him the truth. Give each one of your subordinates enough attention to let him know you expect him to find ways to improve himself and his work.

For instance, if you know an employee is coming in late several times a week, let him know that you're aware of that. Tell him you expect him to correct this fault and that it will be an item for consideration and your personal attention on his next performance report if he doesn't.

If You Do Like a Man's Work, Tell Him That, Too

While you're looking for trouble, though, don't neglect to tell your satisfactory employees that they're doing a good job and that you are happy and well pleased with their efforts. Praise them for their performance and try to help them grow.

"Properly handled, praise can be one of your most potent motivating factors for a man to do even a better job for you," says Hubert Riebold, Foreman in the Industrial Belt Division of the Gates Rubber Company, Denver, Colorado. "I've found it to be really helpful when I praise someone in his weakest area—where he's sincerely trying to do a better job.

"I've also found that it's a good idea to save my praise and a pat on the back for a particularly hard piece of work that a man has handled especially well."

How to Praise a Man Properly

At first glance, this doesn't seem hard to do. In fact, it would seem like the easiest thing in the world to give a man a pat on the back. But there's more to praise than just appealing to a person's vanity or trying to flatter him. For the best results you ought to avoid superlatives like "the very best . . . without parallel . . . impossible to top this . . ." and the like. He'll be liable to suspect your sincerity.

For instance, I once received an army commendation medal. The citation used such words as "superior . . . outstanding . . . exemplary . . . without equal . . . unsurpassed . . . highest possible . . ." and so on. I didn't recognize myself! I thought I was reading about someone else. And to tell the truth, I couldn't figure out, if I really was that good, why I was still a second lieutenant after a year when all the rest of my contemporaries had been promoted to first lieutenant at the end of six months!

You'd be much better off to praise a man using words that come naturally to you, perhaps such phrases as "Good work, George . . . you were never better, Sam . . . excellent job, Al; thanks." They'll be much more likely to believe you.

I'm not implying you should hand out compliments sparingly or grudgingly but don't say something nice to a man if you don't really mean it. Be sincere. Say what you mean and mean what you say.

If a man is doing his level best and comes through for you in a pinch, you don't have to gush all over him like an oil well. Just let him know that you do appreciate his efforts a great deal. Sometimes you're better off just saying, "Thanks."

One last small recommendation here. That is, never praise a man by comparing his work with that of someone else. Always praise him by comparing him with himself. You can best do that by saying how this week's work was better than last week's—that sort of thing. To praise a man by comparing him with someone else will cause nothing but bitterness and hard feelings, for there'll always be those who are lesser or greater than he is.

Tell Him About Company Plans

Bring your people up to date constantly on new developments and future projects. Let them know ahead of time when changes are to be made. As members of your team, they're entitled to know what's going on, too.

Give them enough information about conditions and events in your department, your company, and the industry as a whole, so they can see themselves and their work in the proper perspective.

Let Your Close Assistants in on Your Plans at an Early Stage

I realize some plans can't be discussed far in advance with all your people. They should, however, be gone over as much as possible with your major subordinates before you take final action.

Such advance information will give them an all-important sense of participation. Not only that; since they'll be taking part in making those plans, they'll be anxious to see that they succeed. They'll feel a sense of personal responsibility. As a result, they'll carry out *your* plans with vigor and enthusiasm.

How to Eliminate Misunderstandings

A great many misunderstandings can come about from simple lack of information. For instance, John Green gets a two-week paid vacation. But George Smith, who works right beside him, gets three weeks with full pay. No problem, if John has been told that when he's here ten years just as George has been, he'll get a three-week paid vacation, too.

Joe Brown feels he's been mistreated because he bought some tires for his car from the company and they charged him cost plus ten percent. Joe thought he was getting cheated, but he hadn't listened closely enough during his initial orientation as a new employee. He'd heard only the one word—*cost*. He'd missed the phrase, *plus ten percent.*

Most of the time such complaints come from a simple lack of information. Sometimes management is at fault for not telling the employees what's going on. At other times, employees are wrong for not paying attention, not listening, not reading the bulletin board, and so on. Whatever the reason, see that the misunderstanding is straightened out promptly and satisfactorily.

Let Them Know of Any Changes That Will Affect Them

You don't have to reveal company secrets, but you have a moral obligation to let people know of any planned changes that will affect their security, their income, or their future. It's one way you can show your concern for your employees' welfare.

For instance, if changes in your company will create a new position in a department other than your own for which one of your men is qualified, tell him about it. He's entitled to the chance to better himself.

You might handicap your operation temporarily by losing a good man, but you'll benefit in the long run. And if he doesn't get the job, at least he'll be grateful to you for having given him the chance to try for it. If he misses, he'll appreciate your thoughtfulness and probably do an even better job for you than before.

Let Them Know of Any Changes That Will <u>Not</u> Affect Them

Just as it's important to let a man know when certain changes are going to affect him, it's just as important—in fact, sometimes even more so—to let him know when contemplated changes are *not* going to affect him. Here's a glaring example of how things can go wrong by failing to follow this simple rule.

"Seemingly out of a clear blue sky last summer we started getting all kinds of complaints from our production employees," says Warren Roland, Industrial Relations Director for a large electric appliance manufacturer in St. Louis, Missouri. "They grumbled about bad lighting, poor ventilation, excessive heat, noise, etc. As each problem was satisfactorily resolved, they'd come up with another one.

"This was extremely unlike our people, for we've always enjoyed extremely cordial relations with our employees, so I called in one of the men who's been with us a long time to find out what was really at the bottom of all these complaints.

"Well, their real problem was the fear they were going to be the victims of automation and lose their jobs. You see, we'd had a professional leasing firm in to survey our plant with the idea of selling the building to them and then renting it back on a long-term lease. That way we could free a lot of money for expansion purposes that was tied up in our physical plant.

"But the sudden and unexplained appearance of a lot of snoopers with pencils and notebooks had aroused our employees' suspicions. They were dead certain they were going to be replaced with more machines. Once the reason for all the strangers was explained, the complaints stopped."

You can get this kind of static, too, unless you go all out to keep such misunderstandings from happening. When things go wrong, remember that a few well-placed questions from you to your employees can often quickly clear the air.

Have Your People Tell You What You Have to Hear

I know this chapter has been aimed primarily at keeping your own employees informed, but I want to conclude by saying that the flow of information has to go up as well as down to be completely effective.

One of the most important things your employees can ever do for you is to tell you the truth, too—to let you know what's actually going on in your own shop.

I learned this lesson from an old foreman who told me, "Don't let your employees tell you what you *want* to hear. Let your wife do that. Make 'em tell you what you *have* to hear. That's the only way you can be sure of keeping your job."

That advice proved valuable to me; it could be valuable to you, too.

TWENTY-ONE

Failing to Treat Your Subordinates As Individuals

Industrial psychologists say that one of the biggest mistakes managers can make is to treat their employees like machines or equipment; in other words, *not treating their subordinates as individuals.*

Let's face it. Not a single one of the people who work under you wants to be a nobody. Every last one of them wants to be somebody. No one wants to be just another number—some faceless or nameless anonymity. *Everyone wants to retain his own special individual identity.*

Unfortunately, in today's highly automated and mechanized business and industrial world, a person often does become merely another piece of office equipment or an extension of some part of the machinery.

And then, to make it even worse, since computers depend on numbers rather than names for credit, identification, and billing purposes, each person tends to be converted into a nonentity, even when he's off the job, more than ever before. Today, people just don't seem to be as important as individuals as they used to be.

What does all this mean to you as a manager? Well, it means *you ought to do everything in your power to individualize your workers,* just as Armond Dunlap, Plant Manager for Emerson Electric in St. Louis, does.

"We do everything we can think of to treat our employees as individuals," Mr. Dunlap says. "And since a man's name is more individual and distinctive about him than anything else, that's where we start.

"I insist that every division head and section chief, every single foreman and supervisor, knows the names of all his subordinates. We also provide desk or bench name plates at company cost, so our employees will know they're recognized as valued members of our company—not just faceless names or numbers on a payroll.

"We publish a small weekly plant newspaper that carries news about our employees. Of course, we print news events of plant achievements, special events, promotions, and so on. If we have a new piece of equipment, I have the operator's picture taken with it to go in our company paper. The personnel section also keeps a record of birthdays. When one of our people has a birthday, a notice goes up on the bulletin board and in the paper wishing him 'Many happy returns.' He also gets the day off with full pay.

"Whenever awards are given out, we have a photographer take a picture of the person and his immediate supervisor giving him the award. That gets two employees into the act. Both of them get a copy of the photograph. Another one goes on all the plant bulletin boards. We print the picture and carry the story in our plant newspaper. We also send a picture along with the story to one of our local newspapers.

"But we don't stop with events in the plant. We also carry information about people getting married, children being born, graduation of sons and daughters from high school and college, excelling in sports, drama, etc. Entry into the service, return from the army, that sort of thing is covered, too. The important point is to get the employee's name or the name of a member of his family into our paper, no matter how.

"Is all this worth it? You bet it is. All I have to do is look at our production records and our employee grievance files *before and after* we started using this procedure of treating our employees as individuals. The proof of how well it works for us is all right there."

The important point to keep in mind here is that *all your employees need individual recognition, too.* You'll find, just as Mr. Dunlap did, that when you give them that individual recognition and attention they need so much, you'll raise their morale and get them to do a better all-around job for you.

In fact, when you treat your employees as important individuals . . .

YOU'LL GAIN THESE BENEFITS

1. All your employees will be your friends.
2. None of them will be your enemies.
3. They'll admire and respect you.
4. They'll do what you want them to do.
5. Production will go up; costs, expenses, employee grievances will go down.
6. You'll have influence and power with them that works like magic for you.

TECHNIQUES YOU CAN USE TO GAIN THESE BENEFITS

How to Treat Your Subordinates As Individuals

All sorts of studies have shown that morale and on-the-job performance of the average worker is higher when his boss takes a personal interest in him and treats him as an important individual.

Most managers will admit that it's vital to make their employees feel important—but they don't take the time to do so. They're much too busy with more important things, they say, so they go right on ignoring their people and paying no attention to them. The result? Morale nosedives; so does production. Absenteeism goes up; so do employee grievances.

But it just is not really difficult to treat your people as individuals. Besides, it doesn't take much time. Fifteen or twenty minutes invested daily in the beginning can save you countless hours of listening to formal labor grievances or sitting in nonproductive, unprofitable arbitration hearings. There are three extremely simple ways you can get to know your employees better and make them feel important as individuals at the same time:

1. Know Each Man by His First Name

A man's name is the most important word in all the world to him. To use it can often work what seems like *white magic*.

But if you don't call him by name, if you don't even know his name, if you forget it or mispronounce it, this will work in reverse for you: like *black magic*.

As a good manager, you should be able to call every single one of your employees, not only by their last, but by their first names as well. It's one of the most powerful, most convincing ways you can say to a man: *I recognize you as an important individual*.

"Today I know every single person in the plant by his first name," says Jim Wilkins, President of Kimberly Music Industries, a company in Chicago employing nearly 500 people.

"Oh, I miss once in a while, especially if he's real new, but not very often. But it wasn't always that way. Used to be, I never paid any attention at all to my employees. I knew the main department heads—figured that was enough.

"One day I saw a bunch of men standing around doing nothing. I went up to them, chewed them out for loafing on the job, and told them to get back to work. Told them I hadn't hired them to stand around and if that was all they could find to do, I'd fire them.

"Well, they just laughed at me. So did all the people watching. That made it even worse. I became furious and really blew my stack. Made a complete fool out of myself in front of all my employees.

"Come to find out they didn't even work for me! You see, we lease the building and the landlord had sent some electrical workers over to repair the heating system. They were waiting for their own foreman to tell them what to do.

"Since then, I've kept everything on a personal first-name basis here. I know every one of my people. It's paid off for me in friendship, loyalty, cooperation, and quality production."

If you want the same kind of results for yourself, then treat your employees as people—not cattle. There's a lot of difference between a *team* and a *herd*. People want to be known by their names, not by their clock numbers, "Hey you!", or "Fellas." It doesn't cost you a penny to call a man by his first name, but it makes him feel like a million bucks.

2. Praise Him—Pat Him on the Back

Charles Schwab, a million-dollar-a-year employee of Andrew Carnegie, the steel magnate—and that was back when a dollar was still worth a dollar—knew this secret of how to get the best out of people.

"I look at my ability to arouse enthusiasm among men as the greatest asset I possess," Mr. Schwab said, in effect. "As far as I'm concerned, the only way to inspire a man to do his best is by individual appreciation, praise, and encouragement.

"There is nothing in the world that destroys a man's ambitions as much as criticism. So I never criticize anyone. I believe in giving a man an incentive and a reason to work. I am anxious to praise, but I am always hesitant to find fault. *I am always hearty in my approbation and lavish in my praise.*"

To praise a man for his efforts is not a brand-new idea. Psychological studies conducted in schools, universities, factories, and business firms over the years have also shown conclusively that 95 out of every 100 persons respond far better to praise than they do to criticism.

I, too, have yet to meet the person who doesn't appreciate a compliment or a pat on the back for what he's done. A compliment brings sunshine into a cloudy day. My wife's beauty operator, Carolyn Webb, says, "I can lose more weight with a compliment from my husband about how good I look than I ever can with my doctor's threat of a heart attack!"

"It is actually quite easy to find something to compliment in a person," says George Dwyer, local store manager in Omaha, Nebraska, for Fairfax Fashions, a prominent mid-west chain of clothing stores.

"All you have to do is try. For instance, you can say, 'You handled that difficult customer beautifully, Marge. . . . That's really a brilliant idea, Tom. . . . I sure do appreciate your getting this report in on time, Sam. . . . Thanks for getting those letters out today, Sally. . . .'

"As I say, it's easy. All depends on what you're looking for. If you want to compliment a person, you can always find something to praise him for. If you want to criticize him, you can always find something wrong, too. But I'd rather compliment him than criticize. I find it's a much better way to motivate my employees to do their best for me."

You can find something worth while to praise in your people, too. For instance, does an employee of yours keep an exceptionally clean work bench? Tell him so. Does he have an outstanding safety record? Let him know how much you appreciate that. Has he come up with some labor-saving device or money-making idea? Reward him in some way for his efforts. Is his attendance record exceptional? Is he always on time? Then thank him for that; show him that you care. Is he particularly skilled in his job? Tell him how lucky you are to have him as an employee.

And whenever you can, praise him in public. He'll feel extra special when you do. For instance, have you ever been introduced by your boss to a visitor this way? "Want you to meet Tom Smith. He's one of our best supervisors, a real comer. We're really looking for great things from him."

How do you feel when your boss talked about you this way to someone else? Made you want to go all out for him, right? *That's the power of public praise.*

Your employees feel the same way you do. Everybody responds to praise and a pat on the back. That's human nature. So remember, the second way to treat your subordinate as an individual and make him feel important is to *praise him and compliment him for his efforts.*

3. Show Respect for His Knowledge and His Skill

"One of the best ways I know of to treat an employee as an individual is to show respect for his knowledge and his skill," says Paul Atwood, General Foreman for the Phelps Dodge Corporation in Ajo, Arizona.

"For instance, just yesterday I was watching one of our machine operators, Walter Brown. I marveled at the smoothness of his actions: the sure, deft, rhythmic way he handled his raw materials and his equipment. And I told him so. I said, 'Walter, you absolutely amaze me. Why, I'd never in the world be able to do that as well as you do.'

"Walter looked up at me from his bench and grinned. 'Well, I should hope not,' he said. 'If you could, I might find myself out of a job!'

"Now I sincerely meant what I said to Walter. I do have a deep respect for his abilities, his knowledge, and his skills. I want him to know that I do. But if I don't tell him, he'll never know how I feel."

As Will Rogers used to say, "Everybody's ignorant, 'cept

on different things." Chances are, every person you supervise knows more about his own individual operation than you do. That's the way it should be.

So if you want to make your employee feel good, if you want to treat him as an individual and make him feel important, then remember to use this third step: *Show respect for his knowledge and his skill.*

Make an Honest Effort to Really Know Your People

If you want to treat your employees as individuals, *you'll have to really know them as individuals.* You'll need to know each one's personal idiosyncrasies, his peculiar little quirks. You'll want to know his likes and dislikes—what turns him on and what turns him off.

Pick any employee at random. Do you know what makes him different from the others? Do you understand his particular traits, his basic attitudes, his personal sensitivities, his deep-seated needs and desires?

If you don't, then I'd recommend you do as George Underwood, Production Superintendent for the Pillsbury Company in New Albany, Indiana, does.

"So that I can really know the people who work for me, I keep a photographic album by department," George says. "Each man gets as many pages as necessary. I keep his photograph, his name, the names of his wife and children, their pictures, too, if I can get them, and all the personal details I've been able to gather about him: what his hobbies are, how he spends his leisure time, his likes and dislikes. I'm not snooping or checking up on him. I just want to find out what really makes him tick.

"How do I get the information? *By asking him;* I've found that's the best way. I make it a point to talk to at least five men each day when I make my rounds of the plant. But before I make my daily inspection tour, I check my photograph album first. I review all the facts and details about the men I'm going to talk to that day.

"You see, I don't just talk to the people at random. It might look as if I do, and of course, I want it to look that way. But you can bet I've picked out the people for the day's conversations well in advance. And reviewing their files first keeps me from making a lot of stupid mistakes or hurting someone's feelings. It's the best way I know of to treat my employees as individuals and make them feel important."

Perhaps you wouldn't want to go this far in your efforts to really know your people. If you don't, then at least you ought to keep a notebook with each subordinate's name listed in it. You ought to be able to turn to any employee's page and find his age, his wife's name, how many children he has, their names, his hobbies, how long he's worked for you, something about his background, and other pertinent information about him.

Whichever method you use, you should be able to answer the following questions about every single one of your employees:

1. What does he like to talk about?
2. What are his goals, his ambitions, his objectives?
3. What are his personal characteristics?
4. What is he proud of?
5. How does he accept praise?
6. How does he take criticism?
7. What personal mannerisms does he have?
8. How does he react to challenges?
9. Does he ever come up with good usable ideas?
10. How does he get along with others?
11. What does he complain about?
12. What makes him laugh?

If you can't answer every one of those questions about each and every one of your people who work under you, then whatever system you're using isn't adequate; it's not broad enough in its coverage or scope. You'll need to expand it if you really want to know your people as individuals.

Match His Talents to the Job

When you know everything there is to know about each individual, you will be better able to match his talents to the job. When you know what each person wants individually, you can help him get it.

I realize you cannot always tailor-make a job to precisely fit a man's abilities and desires. But if you can make his work as personal as possible for him, chances are he'll do a much better job for you.

If there is absolutely no resemblance between the job's requirements and what your employee wants or expects from it, he'll perform poorly and be unhappy. When you know what he's best fitted for, you may be able to move him to a job that better matches his talents and abilities.

Recognize each person as an individual and treat him that way. You'll find that you've motivated him to do a better job. You'll have increased his self-confidence and you'll have added direction to his career.

I know there is no magic formula that you can use to guarantee results, but I also know that when you treat every person as an individual—when you make every single person important to you—the morale, efficiency, and productivity of your organization cannot help but go up, and that makes all your extra efforts well worth while.

TWENTY-TWO

Refusing to Train an Assistant to Take Your Place

Ever see a man get promoted who was not as qualified as someone else for the job? Ever wonder why? Has it happened to you, too?

For instance, just pretend you're the big boss yourself and you have four likely candidates for one job. One man is more qualified than all the rest. Would you promote him? "Of course," you say. "If he were the best qualified of the four, I'd be foolish not to promote him."

If that's all the information you had to go on, I'd agree with you. I'd promote the best qualified man, too. But let's suppose he had no one trained to take his place. Let's say it would leave a gaping managerial hole in your organizational setup if you did promote him. You'd be left with a department or a section unable to function properly if you promoted the best qualified man.

Would you still promote him then? Would you move him to the new job no matter what it did to the rest of your organization? I doubt it; I know I wouldn't. Neither did Arthur Needham, manager of an Akron, Ohio, manufacturing plant.

"I'd received wonderful news," Mr. Needham says. "I was being promoted to vice president in charge of all production for the entire corporation. The corporation president, Mr. Allen, was moving Bert Montgomery, the production superintendent, up to take over my place as plant manager. But he'd left it up to me to pick the new plant production superintendent from one of our five department foremen, all of whom were qualified.

"At first glance, it seemed that Carl Simmons would be the man. He'd been with us longest and had seniority on the others. He was the best administrator of the five; his office records were meticulous. His production figures were always right up there at the top. He seemed to be the most logical choice for the job, but I didn't select him.

"Why not? *Because he had trained no one to take his place; no one in his department could take over his job.* If we were to promote him, we'd have a department floundering around without adequate leadership. That would be unthinkable, for in our plant each department's efficient operation depends on all the others. Materials move through all five before they come out as finished products at the end. If one department ceases to function, the entire plant comes to a standstill.

"Carl had made himself literally indispensable in his foreman's job by not training a man to take his place. By failing to do that, he had limited his own chance for advancement.

"But if we were to promote Leland Schroeder, his department would continue to produce just as before because his assistant foreman, Wade Gearing, could step right into his shoes. The entire plant would continue to function as if nothing had happened, and in the final analysis, that's what really had to come first: efficient plant production.

"So I picked Leland for the job of production superintendent since that would be more beneficial, not only for the entire plant, but also for the whole corporation. I knew that he could eliminate whatever weak points he had quickly enough. In the end he'd be an extremely competent production superintendent. He'd be able to grow on the job."

I would have done the same. I'm sure you would have, too. It makes more sense to promote a *fully* (even though not best) *qualified man,* who will improve himself, and thus insure overall operational continuity and efficiency, than it does to promote the best qualified man, only to end up with a rough and sputtering organization that has a hard time getting the job done.

Don't make the mistake of boxing yourself in and failing to be promoted just because no one will be able to take over your job. Train someone to take your place. When you do . . .

YOU'LL GAIN THESE BENEFITS

You'll Always Be Ready for Promotion

Of course, you have to be ready to assume the duties and responsibilities of your own boss at any time if you want to be promoted when he steps up. You need to know every last detail of his job inside out. But that's only half the story. You've got to have someone trained who can step into your own position whenever that happens. Otherwise, you're likely to be passed over, just as Carl Simmons was. Have a man trained to take your place so that won't happen to you. Then you'll always be ready for promotion.

You'll Have a Man to Run the Place for You in Your Absence

You must have depth in your organization if you want it to function properly in your absence. After all, you can't live in your office 24 hours a day. So develop a good assistant who can run the shop when you're gone. Then, if you do have to leave because of illness, an accident, a much-needed vacation, or whatever, you won't have a nervous breakdown worrying about your job while you're away. You might as well have some peace of mind and enjoy your time off. You can if you have an assistant properly trained to take your place.

You'll Have More Time for Your Other Managerial Duties

Not enough time in the day to get everything done is a common complaint of most industrial managers and business executives. If you try to handle all the details of your job without any help, chances are you'll have to let some things slide by or just give them the broad brush treatment. But when you have an assistant trained to take your place, you can let him take care of some of your managerial duties during your busiest periods. That way you can have some time to take care of those things you've been neglecting.

You Can Devote Some of Your Time to Image-Building Activities

Jerry Williams, a manager of a department store in Portland, Oregon, is taking the lead in a local Community Chest fund drive. So are hundreds of other executives and managers throughout the country.

Arnold Hubbard, Southern Bell Telephone Company manager in Baton Rouge, Louisiana, has been named "Young Man of the Year" by the Junior Chamber of Commerce there. Because of his activities as a telephone executive? No, because of his work in Kiwanis, Boy Scouts, Red Cross, and March of Dimes fund drives. Nor is Arnold Hubbard unique, either. Many, many company and corporation executives and businessmen give of their time to help the community in which they live.

How are these people able to devote part of their working day to such civic activities that help improve the images of the companies they work for? By making sure they have assistants trained who can "mind the store" for them while they're away.

If you work for a company or corporation yourself, I can assure you that they'll be deeply interested in how good a job you do in promoting their image in your city. With that thought in mind, you'd be well-advised to have someone trained to take your place while you're working on those activities. In the long run, it's to your advantage to do so.

TECHNIQUES YOU CAN USE TO GAIN THESE BENEFITS

Make the Decision to Develop an Assistant to take Your Place

In Chapter Four, we talked about how to make sound and timely decisions. Now it's time for you to put what you learned back there to work, for the first step in developing an assistant to take your place is to *make the decision to do so.*

Some people hit a snag right here at the very beginning, because they're completely unwilling to relax their grip on the reins of responsibility and authority. Any mistake an assistant makes will reflect on them and they don't like that idea.

I'll admit myself that delegation of a piece of work to someone else isn't easy to do. Most of us, myself included, feel we can do the task better than anyone else. So it goes against the grain to hand a job over to someone else to do.

Then there's always the person who thinks the organization will fall completely apart when he leaves it. Like Scott Brady, a retired Air Force colonel who lives down the street from me. "When I left the service I didn't think they could make it without me," Scott says. "But somehow they did. Now the only person who even remembers me after my 28 years' service is the finance officer who sends me my retirement pay check every month, and damned if he isn't an IBM machine!"

So don't get hung up on this first step. Just say to yourself, *"What will happen if I don't train an assistant to take my place?"* Then write down the possibilities. You've already seen what happened to Carl Simmons. I assume you don't want that to happen to you.

Now ask yourself, *"What will happen if I do develop an assistant to take my place?"* Write down these possibilities, too. I've already given you a hint of the good things that can come your way in the section called "You'll Gain These Benefits."

I'm sure, when you compare the advantages and disadvantages of these two courses of action, you'll be ready to make your decision. Do so. Don't procrastinate; there's no reason to put it off. Make the decision today to develop someone to take your place.

How to Pick the Right Person for the Job

How can you know if you're picking the right person? Well, of course, you won't have the final answer until he works at the job for a while. But you can stack the deck in your favor by checking him out thoroughly first.

For example, if he's to be promoted from within the organization, you should've had a chance to watch his work over a period of time. You can always go through his personnel file and read over his performance reports. You can also test him by giving him some trial management assignments to see how well he does before you make your final decision.

If you hire your assistant from the outside, then you'll have to depend on a personal interview plus a reference check and a talk with his former employees.

"Let me make one small suggestion on how to best pick the right man to be your assistant," says Martin Block, Personnel Director for the Sun Oil Company in Tulsa, Oklahoma. "I know he'll need to possess most of the same basic managerial abilities that you have. But you should try to find a man who *complements* you rather than one who reflects a mirror image of you.

"If the two of you are exactly alike—if you have the same strengths and weaknesses—there'll be sparks flying in no time. The assistant who'll work best with you will be the one whose strengths match your weaknesses and whose weak points match your strong ones. That way, you'll mesh with each other rather than clash."

Qualities You Should Look For in an Assistant

You shouldn't expect to find a well-trained assistant who can move right in and take over without any help at all from you. You'll want to work with him and train him yourself.

What kind of person should he be? Well, hopefully, he'll be the kind who'll be willing to learn from your experience so he won't have to make the same mistakes that you made. He should also be the sort of person who can learn fast and who is anxious to get ahead.

You'll want someone who can think for himself—one who has some plain old everyday common sense, too. He should have the ability to work with people, to get along with them, to gain their trust and confidence. And he must be willing to accept responsibility. Finally, he'll need the initiative and ingenuity of a leader, for he'll be representing you in all ways when you're absent.

If he does have these basic qualities a manager needs, you can teach him the special duties and responsibilities of your own particular job. You can also teach him the skills of management that are best learned by practical on-the-job-training; for example, planning, making decisions, supervising the work of others.

How to Delegate Responsibility to Your Assistant

If you want your assistant to do his best for you, you'll have to work closely with him. The actual delegation of some of your responsibilities will be one of your biggest tasks. Here are five methods you can use to make that transition of power as smooth and easy as possible.

1. Give him a complete picture of the job.   See that your assistant has the necessary information he needs to fulfill his duties and responsibilities. Give him a clear and accurate picture of exactly what you want him to do. Let him know precisely where his authority begins and ends.

Make certain your people know his exact status, too. They must understand clearly that they are to deal directly with him and not with you from now on. If you don't make that a hard and fast rule—to be broken only in extreme emergencies— you'll be defeating your purpose in developing an assistant to help you. If you do make that point clear to your subordinates, they'll cooperate with him.

2. Let him know what you're doing.   If he's to do a good job for you, you must also keep him advised at all times about what you're doing. Tell him about your plans, their progress, and the reasons for your decisions, your actions, and your orders. He should also be made aware of problems as they come up. Let him solve them for you. Share your knowledge and experience with him, so he can learn the ins and outs of working with people as well as the intricate and intimate details of your job.

3. Add responsibility gradually.   Don't load everything on him at once. Let him get the feel of the job first. Add to his duties gradually as he learns the ropes. If you assign him additional responsibilities in small doses, he'll learn to take care of them as he goes along. He'll grow in ability and become a competent managerial assistant to you.

4. Don't hold a tight checkrein on him.   Some managers try to keep their fingers on each and every tiny detail that takes place in their area of operation. That's impossible to do. This constant checking on subordinates harasses them. It makes people nervous and will actually slow down their work.

It's far better to give a man a job to do and let him do it. Get out of the way and let him work. Then have him report back to you when the job is done. Let him tell you how it went; help him correct any mistakes he made so he can do it better the next time. That way he'll grow in his ability to do the job for you.

5. Give him the authority he needs to carry out his responsibility.   If you're going to hold him responsible for getting the job done, you'll have to give him the authority to do it. Encourage him to bring problems to you only when something seems radically wrong or when he's at his wit's end to solve it himself. Get him to bring along one or more suggested solutions to the problem, too. Then help him grow by steering him toward the proper decision—but let him make that decision himself. That is your duty and his right.

A Final Bit of Advice

"Just the fact that you're a manager doesn't mean you have to end each day in total exhaustion and every week on the verge of a nervous breakdown," says Steve Powers, Production Foreman for the Westinghouse Electric Company in Tampa, Florida. "But that can happen to you if you try to do it all alone. You'll last a lot longer and go a lot further when you let your people help carry your load.

"Developing an assistant to take your place can make your job a lot simpler for you. An assistant can give you the time you need to think, to plan, to meet emergencies, to solve problems, and to relax a little. He can make life a lot easier and much more pleasant for you."

You'll last a lot longer and go a lot further, too, with a competent and trusted assistant to fill in for you. You can take some time off to do things with your family and your friends. In short, the proper assistant, after he's trained to take your place, can help you to enjoy a fuller and richer life, both at work and at home.